ALIENS

MARVELS & MYSTERIES

ALIENS

•PARRALLEL•

This material has previously appeared in
partwork form as *The Unexplained*

Published in 1995 by Parrallel
Unit 13-17 Avonbridge Trading Estate,
Atlantic Road, Avonmouth, Bristol BS11 9QD

ISBN 0-75251-217-X

Printed and bound in Singapore

CONTENTS

Introduction

Since the 1950s an increasing number of people from all around the world have made contact with beings – some of them strange and fantastical, others disconcertingly human in appearance – who seemed to be from another world. Some aliens have brought messages of hope for Earth, others have been gloomy harbingers of doom and catastrophe. Some appear to have a scientific bent, taking samples of plants and carrying out medical examinations of people they have abducted, usually from lonely places late at night. Some of them have attacked contactees, others have had sex with them.

This book presents the stories of many of these contactees, and asks the questions that need to be asked. Where do the aliens come from? Are they visitors from other worlds, or from bases hidden deep inside the earth? Are they travellers from the future, or have they always been here, existing in other dimensions that we occasionally glimpse, as it were, out of the corner of our eyes? And what is it that they want with us?

Some people argue that aliens are creations of the human mind, the response of creative imaginations to some natural, outside stimulus that we do not yet quite understand. Others are convinced that the aliens are 'visions', created in the contactees' minds by telepathic manipulation across unimaginable reaches of time and space.

This book also attempts to discover how long the aliens have been visiting our planet. Reports of flying saucers and spacemen have proliferated only since the time of World War II, but is it possible that many of our myths and legends, from the warring ancient gods to fairy folk, nature spirits, angels and demons, are part

A NIGHT TO REMEMBER

AFTER BETTY AND BARNEY HILL HAD SEEN A UFO AT CLOSE QUARTERS, BETTY DREAMED SHE HAD BEEN ABDUCTED AND INTIMATELY EXAMINED BY MEMBERS OF AN ALIEN SPECIES

In September 1961, Betty Hill and her husband Barney were taken on board a spacecraft from another world, subjected to examination and given information by the alien crew members. That, at least, was what the Hills believed. Their case is one of many; and more of the same kind are constantly being reported. But the Hills' account is particularly interesting and one of the most fully documented and thoroughly investigated abductions.

Whether their experience was just what it seemed or some kind of fantasy, it is important that we should know exactly what happened to Betty and Barney Hill that night, for it is part of a widespread pattern. The Hills lived at Portsmouth, New Hampshire, in the eastern United States. Barney, who was black, was aged 39 at the time. He worked as a mail sorter in Boston, a job he was glad to have, even though it was somewhat below his capacity and involved not only night work but also a daily car journey of 60 miles (100 kilometres) each way. Outside his work, Barney was known to be active in the campaign for civil rights for blacks. Betty, aged 41, was white and a child welfare worker. Both had been married before and had children by their earlier marriages, though the children were all living with their other parents. To all appearances, it was a happy and successful marriage: the couple were popular and had many friends.

Late on 19 September 1961, the Hills were on their way home after a short holiday trip to Niagara and Montreal. They were driving through the night because they had run low on money, the trip having been undertaken on the spur of the moment. They stopped for a snack at a roadside restaurant, which they left a little after 10 p.m. to drive on down Highway US3. During their journey that night, the Hills passed no other cars and saw only one other person. What happened to the couple on the journey home was described by Betty in a letter to a UFO investigator five days later:

Betty and Barney Hill, below, were returning from a short vacation when they claimed to have seen a UFO during a night drive along a lonely highway in New Hampshire, USA. Two years after the incident, they both began to suffer from chronic ill health and nervous disorders. Betty was also experiencing disturbing dreams and Barney complained of stress, exhaustion and other anxiety symptoms.

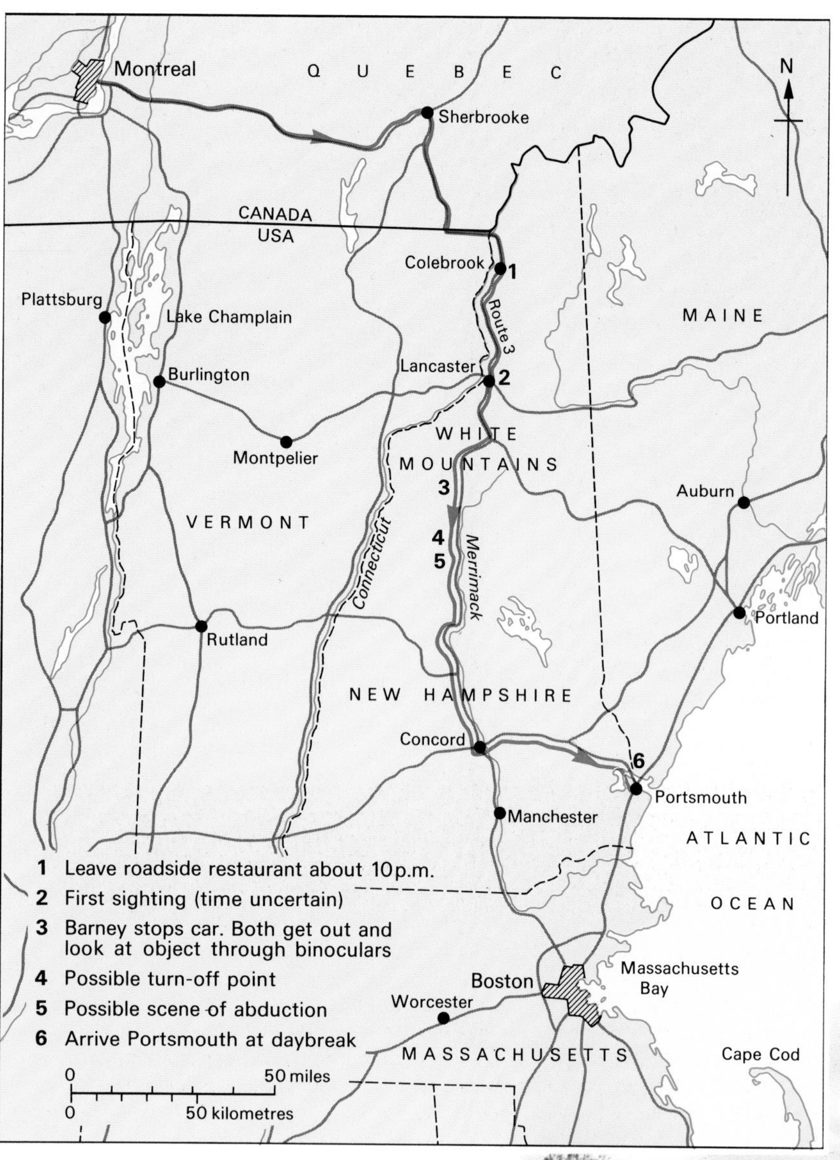

'My husband and I have become immensely interested in this topic [UFOs] as we recently had quite a frightening experience, which does seem to differ from others of which we are aware.

'About midnight on September 20th, we were driving in a National Forest Area in the White Mountains, in N.H. [New Hampshire]. This is a desolate, uninhabited area. At first we noticed a bright object in the sky, which seemed to be moving rapidly. We stopped our car and got out to observe it more closely with our binoculars. Suddenly, it reversed its flight path from the north to the south-west and appeared to be flying in a very erratic pattern. As we continued driving and then stopping to watch it, we observed the following flight pattern: the object was spinning and appeared to be lighted only on one side, which gave it a twinkling effect.

'As it approached our car, we stopped again. As it hovered in the air in front of us, it appeared to be pancake in shape, ringed with windows in the front through which we could see bright blue-white lights. Suddenly, two red lights appeared on each side. By this time, my husband was standing in the road, watching closely. He saw wings protrude on each side and the red lights were on the wing tips.

'As it glided closer, he was able to see inside this object, but not too closely. He did see several figures scurrying about as though they were making some hurried type of preparation. One figure was observing us from the windows. From the distance this was seen, the figures appeared to be about the size of a pencil and seemed to be dressed in some type of shiny black uniform.

" Although their occupations do not especially qualify the witnesses as trained scientific observers, I was impressed by their intelligence, apparent honesty, and obvious desire to get at the facts and to underplay the more sensational aspects of the sighting. Hill had been a complete UFO sceptic before the sighting. "

John G. Fuller,

The Interrupted Journey

The route taken by Barney and Betty Hill on the night they saw the UFO is shown **left.**

It was on Highway US3, **below,** *that the Hills stopped their car and got out to look at the flying object. Betty described it as pancake-shaped with windows in the front through which could be seen bright blue-white lights, as illustrated* **right.** *The object also appeared to have fins tipped with red lights.*

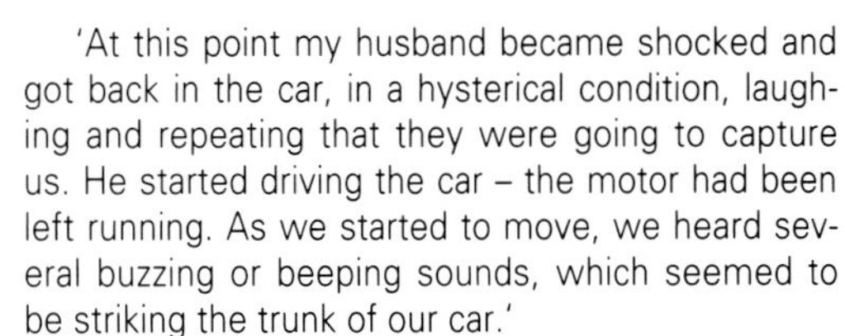

'At this point my husband became shocked and got back in the car, in a hysterical condition, laughing and repeating that they were going to capture us. He started driving the car – the motor had been left running. As we started to move, we heard several buzzing or beeping sounds, which seemed to be striking the trunk of our car.'

This letter, written to Donald Keyhoe of the National Investigations Committee for Aerial Phenomena (NICAP), effectively summarises what the Hills remembered of their experience. But what it lacks is the emotional response of the couple, more vividly described by John G. Fuller in his definitive account of the Hills' experience, entitled *The Interrupted Journey.*

Missing Time Puzzle

It was not until 25 November, two months later, in the course of questioning by UFO investigators, that a 'missing time' puzzle emerged. Here are Barney's own words: 'They were mentally reconstructing the whole trip. One of them said: "What took you so long to get home?" They said: "You went this distance and it took you these hours. Where were you?" Well, when they said this, I thought I was really going to crack up... I became suddenly flabbergasted to think that I realised for the first time that at the rate of speed I always travel, we should have arrived home at least two hours earlier than we did.'

The Hills had taken seven hours to travel 190 miles (305 kilometres), on empty roads, often at 65-70 miles per hour (105-112 km/h).

Ten days after their return, Betty started to experience a series of disturbing dreams. By this time, she had already written her letter to Major Keyhoe, quoted earlier, but had not yet been visited by any investigator. She had told friends and relatives about the experience and was not just puzzled but very disturbed by it. Not surprisingly, her dreams reflected her anxiety.

But they did more than that. While taking the UFO sighting as a starting point, her dreams seemed to continue the incident. In fact, they present a highly detailed account of happenings that, though extremely bizarre, follow on logically from the sighting itself.

Betty's own account of her dreams is included as an appendix to Fuller's book. But unfortunately, he does not indicate when the notes were made; nor does he make it clear how many dreams there were, and whether they repeated the same material, or whether some of the story was contained in each, as fragments that Betty later combined to form a coherent narrative. In other words, we cannot be sure that the smooth, continuous flow of her narrative was also a characteristic of the dreams themselves, or whether it was the result of her own re-telling of the dreams. In the light of subsequent events, the coherence and detail of Betty's account of her dreams are of crucial significance.

The dream experience begins at a point immediately following the UFO sighting. Betty sees a very sharp left-hand turn in the road, which then turns back to the right. A group of eight or eleven men are standing in the middle of the road. Barney

> "One writer has intimated that the Hills are obviously emotionally ill... it seems clear that it was the experience that caused the emotional imbalance, and not the emotional imbalance that caused the experience."
>
> **T. M. Wright, *An Intelligent Man's Guide to Flying Saucers***

slows down, and the motor dies. As he tries to start the motor, the men surround the car. The couple sit motionless and speechless. Betty is terrified. The men open the car doors, reach in and take Barney and Betty by the arm.

Next, Betty seems to be walking along a path in the woods, with men ahead of, beside and behind her. Barney is similarly accompanied. She speaks to him but he does not seem to hear her: it is as though he is sleepwalking. The man on Betty's left, hearing her say Barney's name, asks if that is his name. She does not answer. He tries to assure her that there is nothing to be frightened of, and that no harm will come to them.

Soon they reach a small clearing, where a disc-shaped craft is parked. Betty described it as 'almost as wide as my house is long'. There are no lights or windows to be seen. They climb a ramp towards a door in the craft and, reluctantly, Betty goes in. They then emerge into a corridor, curving with the shape of the disc. Betty is taken into the first room opening off the corridor, but Barney is led further along. When Betty objects, the leader explains that only one person at a time can be tested in each room, and that it will be quicker to examine them separately .

The men leave Betty in the room and a pleasant, reassuring man, who speaks English, enters: he is the examiner. He asks several questions about her age, her diet and so on. Then he makes her sit on a stool while he carries out a superficial inspection, taking samples of hair and ear wax, fingernail clippings and scrapings from her skin.

Next, he asks Betty to lie down on a table. He examines her with a machine that has needles on the end of wires. This, he explains, is to check her nervous system. During this test, her dress is removed. With a needle 4 to 6 inches (10 – 15 centimetres) long, the examiner carries out what he calls a pregnancy test, which consists of jabbing the needle into her navel. The test is extremely painful, but the leader, who has returned to the room to watch the examination, clears the pain by waving his hand before Betty's eyes. She senses his concern, and from this point loses all fear of him.

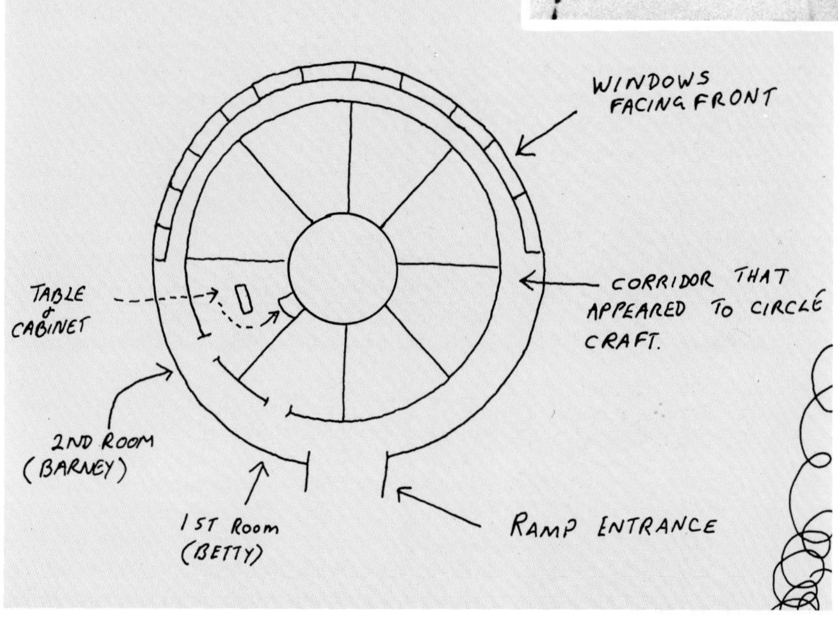

That concludes the testing, and the examiner leaves to help with Barney, whose testing is taking longer. Alone with the leader, Betty examines the room and begins to chat with him. He apologises for frightening her and offers to answer her questions.

They are interrupted when some of the men enter. After a brief conversation, the leader turns to Betty, opens her mouth, and touches her teeth as though trying to move them. He is puzzled by the fact that Barney's teeth are movable while Betty's are not; so Betty explains about Barney's dentures. This leads to a discussion of old age, which the man seems not to comprehend, for he asks Betty about time and how it is measured.

Betty asks for some proof of the incident. The leader agrees; and when she looks round the room and sees a book, he says she may take it. Discussion of the book leads to questions about the Universe; and the leader pulls out a kind of map

Barney, top, shows his drawing of the spacecraft as he remembered seeing it – with fins either side, tipped with red lights, and members of the alien crew looking out of the windows. Although he had no conscious memory of being abducted, he was able – after hypnosis – to draw the plan, above, of the arrangement of rooms inside the craft, and sketched the area, top left, where the craft landed. His diagram shows the Hills' car on the highway and the group of spacemen (shown as dots) who abducted the couple.

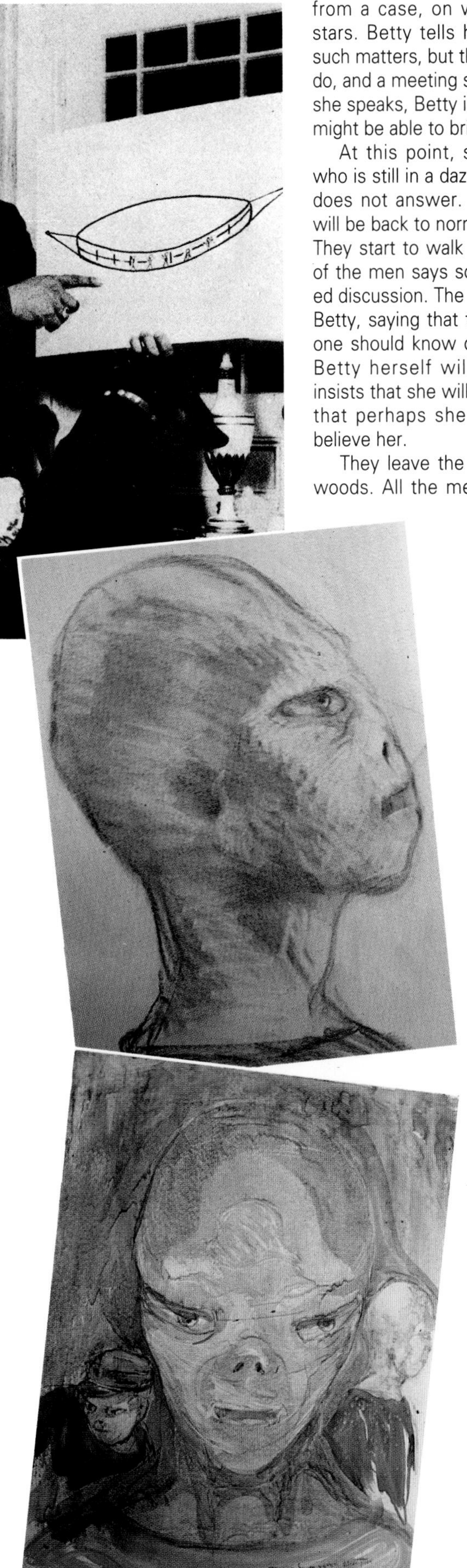

from a case, on which are marked a number of stars. Betty tells him that she knows little about such matters, but that there are others on Earth who do, and a meeting should be arranged with them. As she speaks, Betty is wondering whether she herself might be able to bring about such a meeting.

At this point, some men return with Barney, who is still in a daze. When Betty speaks to him, he does not answer. The leader assures her that he will be back to normal when they return to their car. They start to walk towards the door, and then one of the men says something that provokes an excited discussion. The leader takes the book away from Betty, saying that the rest of the crew feel that no one should know of this experience and that even Betty herself will not remember it. When she insists that she will remember somehow, he agrees that perhaps she will, but he says nobody will believe her.

They leave the disc and walk back through the woods. All the men accompany them. Betty tells the leader she is happy about meeting him and begs him to return. He says it is possible, but he cannot say for certain.

The artist's impressions of the alien crew of the spacecraft,* left, *are based on the Hills' verbal descriptions. In Betty's dreams, the aliens put the couple into separate rooms aboard their craft and carried out physical examinations.

Barney seems to become more alert once they approach the car, but shows no emotion and behaves as though this were an everyday occurrence. They get into the car. The disc becomes a bright glowing object, seems to roll like a ball, turns over three or four times, and then sails into the sky. Betty turns back to Barney and says it is the most marvellous, most unbelievable experience of her entire life. Barney starts driving. So far he has not uttered a word. She turns to him and asks: 'Do you believe in flying saucers now?' He replies: 'Don't be ridiculous!'

Intriguing though they were, Betty's dreams figured in the case only because they confirmed the impact made on her by the sighting. The investigators who visited the couple were concerned only with the waking experiences reported by the Hills. Walter Webb, an astronomer who served as one of NICAP's scientific advisers, was impressed by the Hills' testimony.

In his report, Webb wrote: 'It is the opinion of this investigator, after questioning these people for over six hours and studying their reactions and personalities during that time, that they were telling the truth, and the incident occurred exactly as reported except for some minor uncertainties and technicalities... I was impressed by their intelligence, apparent honesty, and obvious desire to get at the facts and to underplay the more sensational aspects of the sighting.'

Fears, Real and Imagined

Significantly, Webb went on to observe: 'Mr Hill believes he saw something he doesn't want to remember. He claimed he was not close enough to see any facial characteristics on the figures, although at another time he referred to one of them looking over his shoulder and grinning, and to the leader's expressionless face. However, it is my view that the observer's blackout is not of any great significance. I think the whole experience was so improbable and fantastic to witness – along with the very real fear of being captured adding to imagined fears – that his mind finally refused to believe what his eyes were perceiving and a mental block resulted.'

In the course of the ensuing year, it was Barney's 'mental block' that gradually assumed overwhelming importance. His health deteriorated, and with it his mental state: his ulcer became more pronounced, and he became exhausted and depressed. Seeking a cause, it was not surprising that the Hills should wonder whether their UFO experience had played any part in it. They suggested this to their doctor, who proposed hypnosis as a means of discovering more about the sighting and its effect on them. Already, during the investigation of their story, hypnosis had been proposed as a means of acquiring further data, so the Hills welcomed the suggestion.

But Betty had an additional reason for seeking what hypnosis might reveal: 'The moment they suggested hypnosis, I thought of my dreams, and this was the first time I began to wonder if they were more than just dreams... '

ALIEN REVELATIONS

SENSATIONAL INFORMATION ABOUT ALIEN VISITORS EMERGED WHEN BETTY AND BARNEY HILL'S MEMORIES OF THEIR CLOSE ENCOUNTER WERE PROBED BY HYPNOSIS

Barney and Betty Hill presented themselves at the office of Dr Benjamin Simon on 14 December 1963 to begin a series of hypnosis sessions that was eventually to last seven months. Dr Simon was a practitioner of experience and repute, ideally suited for the task in hand; and his open-minded attitude enabled the troubled couple to present their stories in an atmosphere of sympathetic understanding, free from any risk of bias or prejudice.

It is important to remember why hypnosis was tried. In Betty's words:

Betty and Barney Hill are seen **above**, *under hypnosis during their seven-month course of treatment. Their hypnotherapist – Dr Benjamin Simon,* **right** *– was concerned with 'the cumulative impact of past experiences and fantasies on their present experiences and responses', not with the existence of UFOs. In an introduction to the published account of the case, he was careful to say that hypnosis is a pathway to the truth 'as it is felt and understood by the patient'.*

The artist's impression, **left**, *shows Betty and Barney being led to the mysterious craft by members of its crew. Betty felt great fear at this point, but Barney later insisted he had felt none.*

'We went to Dr Simon to get relief from the emotional trouble, and to determine what its cause was. In other words, we'd gone for medical help, not to find out about a UFO experience.'

The sessions were not part of a wider course of psychoanalysis, but were designed to see what relevance the alleged UFO sighting might have had to Barney's physical and psychological state. They therefore do not give us a general picture of the couple's psychological background. Indeed, there are many questions we would like answered about them – about their attitudes to such matters as their interracial marriage, their previous marriages, their separation from their children, their involvement with social work and civil rights, for instance, all of which could have some bearing on how we evaluate their story. But no such information is forthcoming: Dr Simon's probing, and his subsequent comments, were limited to the task in hand.

Each subject was hypnotised separately, with the other out of the room, one after the other. They did not hear each other's sessions at the time, nor the tapes of their own sessions. Only when Dr Simon judged that he had accomplished all he could and had brought the sessions to an end did he invite the couple to hear the tapes for the first time. They chose to listen to them together.

All this was done at the Hills' own instigation. Apart from the emotional ordeal, seven months of sessions with a consultant of the highest qualifications must have cost a great sum of money. So there must have been an exceedingly strong motivation for such a financial burden.

Two Viewpoints

Under hypnosis, the Hills independently told a story that closely matched the dreams that had so troubled Betty in the weeks following their supposed sighting. But there was a difference: the histories were now recounted as the experiences of two people, each describing the events as seen from his or her individual viewpoint. During the phases of the story when the couple were together, each account confirmed the other; but when they were separated, they had their own stories to tell, and told them with an immediacy and intensity that give a vivid impression of re-living an actual experience. According to Barney:

'I started to get out of my car, and put one foot on the ground. And two men were standing beside me, helping me out. I felt very relaxed, yet very frightened. They didn't say anything. I knew I was walking, or moving down the road from the position of where my car was parked. And I could see the ramp that I went up... I could hear a humming sound that they seemed to be making. I was afraid to open my eyes. I had been told not to open my eyes, and it would be over with quickly. And I could feel them examining me with their hands. They looked at my neck, and I could feel them touching my skin right down my back. As if they were counting my spinal column. And I felt something touch right at the base of my spine, like a finger pushing, a single finger.'

Betty's account was equally detailed: 'They led Barney right past the door where I'm standing. So I said: "What are you doing with Barney? Bring him

In Focus

MERELY STAR-STRUCK?

The American UFO sceptic Robert Sheaffer, *right*, declared that the Hills' experience began when they misidentified the planet Jupiter as a UFO. Betty, he explained, first saw a bright 'star' near the Moon; later, a second one appeared and seemed to be moving. Jupiter and Saturn were visible near the Moon that night: and had there been a UFO, Sheaffer said, Betty would have seen three 'stars'. Sheaffer also dismissed Betty's other claims – that the UFO acted 'much like a yo-yo', had passed in front of the Moon in silhouette and flashed 'thin pencils of different-coloured lights, rotating around an object which at that time appeared cigar-shaped'. He cited other cases, too, in which witnesses have produced fantastic misinterpretations of bright stars.

At various times, the Hills put the UFO encounter at around 11 p.m., between midnight and 1 a.m., and at around 3 a.m. Furthermore, Barney recalled that, as the UFO approached them, he drove extremely slowly; and on the homeward journey, he stopped at least once, for reasons he could not remember. Sheaffer insisted that there is so much uncertainty as to the times and their speed of travel that there is no reason to believe in the supposed 'loss' of the two hours – a loss that in any event was discovered only weeks later.

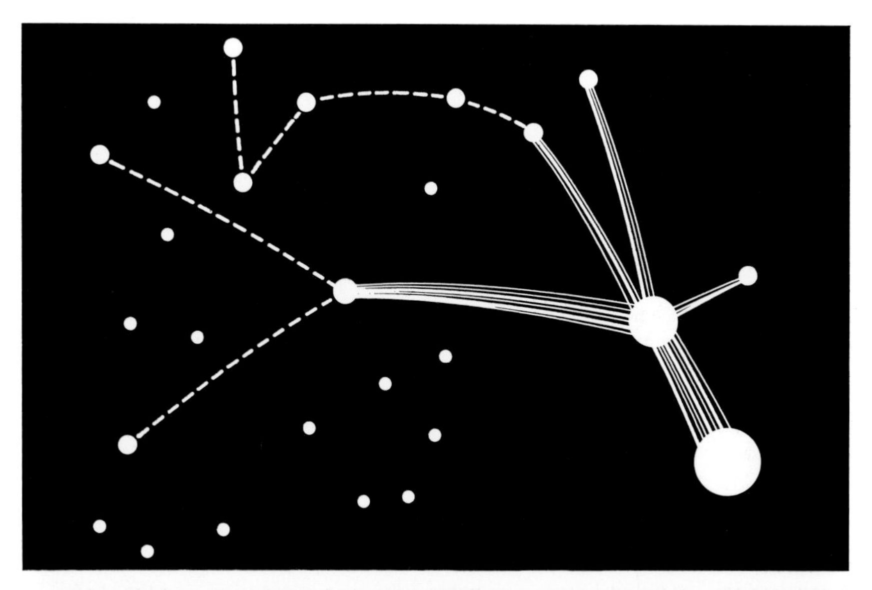

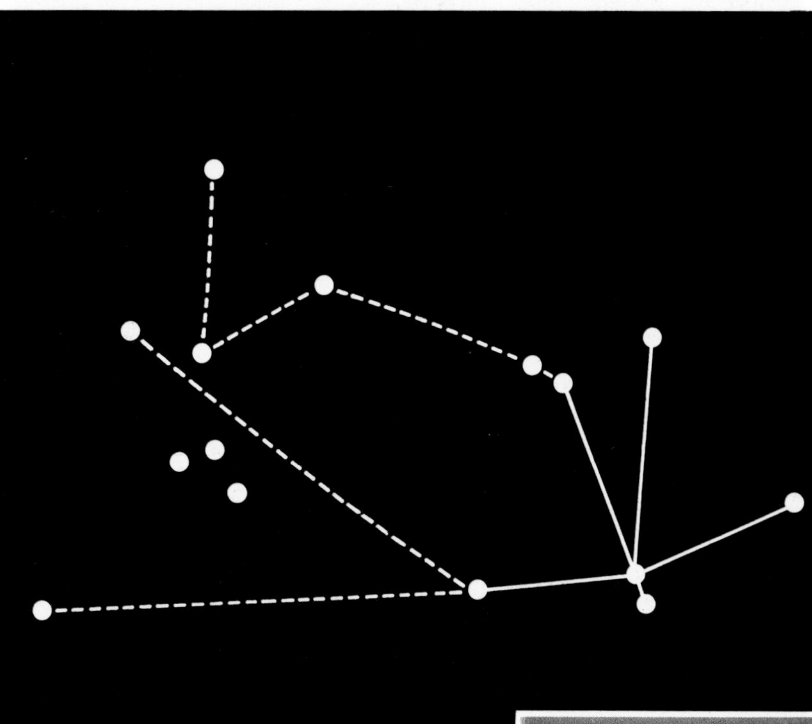

in here where I am." And the man said: "No, we only have equipment enough in one room to do one person at a time. And if we took you both in the same room, it would take too long. So Barney will be all right, they're going to take him into the next room. And then as soon as we get through testing the both of you, then you will go back to your car. You don't have to be afraid."...And they rub – they have a machine, I don't know what it is. They bring the machine over and they put it – it's something like a microscope, only with a big lens. I had an idea they were taking a picture of my skin. And they both looked through this machine... Then they took something like a letter opener and they scraped my arm here, and there was like little – you know how your skin gets dry and flaky sometimes, like little particles of skin? And they put something like a piece of cellophane or plastic, they scraped, and they put this that came off on this plastic.'

Alien Star Map

One of the practical applications of hypnosis is to bring into the conscious mind information that is stored in the subconscious – things experienced but not consciously noted by the witness. This was used to good effect by Dr Simon in connection with the star map that Betty Hill said she had been shown by the 'leader' of the aliens. Dr Simon suggested that, after the session, when she got home, she might care to try to draw what she remembered of the map. To judge from her account, given here, it could have provided a valuable clue as to the origin of her abductors.

'I asked him where he was from. Because I said that I knew he wasn't from the Earth... and he asked if I knew anything about the Universe. And I told him no. I knew practically nothing... And he went across the room... there was an opening. And he pulled out a map... It was an oblong map... And there were all these dots on it... Some were little, just pinpoints. And others were as big as a nickel ... there were curved lines going from one dot to another. And there was one big circle, and it had a lot of lines coming out from it. A lot of lines going to another circle quite close but not as big... And I

" Psychologists generally agree that what a person says while under hypnosis need not necessarily be actual fact but rather represents what the person believes to have happened. Hypnosis is of little value in separating fact from fantasy. "

Robert Sheaffer, The UFO Verdict

***Betty Hill recalled being shown a star map, rather like the one reproduced* top left. *The stars, seen from an unknown viewpoint, form unfamiliar patterns. After several years work, Marjorie Fish arrived at the interpretation, shown* centre left. *The aliens' home system, zeta 1 Reticuli, she believed, is about 37 light-years from us. Marjorie Fish arrived at her result by making a model of stars near the Sun, and using beads mounted on threads, as shown* bottom left.**

asked him what they meant. And he said that the heavy lines were trade routes... the solid lines were places they went occasionally. And he said the broken lines were expeditions... So I asked him where was his home port, and he said: "Where were you on the map?" I looked and laughed, and said: 'I don't know.' So he said: "If you don't know where you are, then there isn't any point of my telling where I am from." And he put the map... back in the space in the wall... '

Betty drew the map to the best of her recollection; but with no names and no points of reference, it was totally meaningless. However, in 1968, a schoolteacher and amateur astronomer, Marjorie Fish, realised that there must be a limited number of actual configurations of stars that would match up to the points on the map. She started by making a three-dimensional model of Betty's map out of beads and string, and then set about seeking a match for it among the not-too-distant stars. After five years, she felt satisfied that she had found such a match.

The illustration* above *shows the Hills' first close-up view of the aliens as they approached the couple's stalled car. This careful reconstruction of Betty and Barney's descriptions appeared in the UFO magazine* Flying Saucer, *after the case had caught the public's imagination.

The Fish map started a controversy almost as lively as that engendered by the Hills' original sighting. An astronomer, Terence Dickinson, was favourably impressed and presented the case for the Fish model in an authoritative article:

'Basically, the Fish interpretation is a view from a few light-years beyond the stars zeta 1 and zeta 2 Reticuli, looking back towards the Sun and the star 82 Eridani, which is about midway between us and the Reticuli pair. The 15 stars shown on the map are all basically like the Sun and could theoretically have planets like Earth. These are the types of stars some astronomers are currently examining in search of signals from alien intelligences. It is therefore a reasonable assumption that this type of star may be the only type on the map... No other interpretation of the Hill map includes all of the solar-type stars within a specific area of space containing the Sun... and makes sense in terms of logical travel between the stars.'

The Fish model provoked much debate, largely related to the chances of finding such a pattern at random among the numerous stars in the neighbourhood of the Sun. By way of testing this, Charles W. Atterberg offered an alternative conjecture as to the region shown in the map. It is a measure of how debatable the findings are that the UFO sceptic Robert Sheaffer should find the Atterberg model superior to the Fish version, whereas Dickinson claims that it is more arbitrary in its selection of stars and contains several inconsistencies.

Predictions Confirmed

Additional support for the Fish model appeared in 1969, when a revised star catalogue, containing information that was simply not available in 1961, was published for the first time and confirmed predictions made by Fish on the basis of the Hill map. Though this is still not definite proof, it is strongly supportive of the Hill-Fish suggestion. But the question remains as to how much reliance can be placed on the recollections, by someone totally unversed in astronomy, of a map seen – under distinctly bizarre conditions – more than two years earlier.

The star map is the most tangible aspect of the Hill case, and lends itself to testing. For the rest, it is a matter of evaluating the Hills' personal testimony, but in the complete absence of any physical evidence – how valuable the book that Betty was offered would have been, if she had only been allowed to bring it away! – evaluation is limited to assessing the credibility of the Hills themselves. No critic has questioned their honesty and sincerity; rather, it is their interpretation of their experience that has to be questioned. It is in this respect that the lack of information about the Hills' personal background becomes important. For it is clear that there are factors in the Hills' personal circumstances that could be very relevant to the way we judge their story. We have already noted such external factors as their previous marriages, and Barney's state of health; and there is also considerable evidence to show that Betty was a much more unusual person than she is generally presented as being.

Barney Hill died in February 1969, five years after the sessions with Dr Simon, of a cerebral haemorrhage, like his father before him. Thereafter, Betty enjoyed the mixed blessings of fame. Her case has been featured in books and magazines, and was even presented as a full-length movie. She made countless public appearances at lectures and conferences, and was a guest on many radio and television shows. Some time after the hypnotic sessions, she gave up her work and devoted herself full-time to UFO research. As something of a celebrity, she was even recognized on the most unlikely occasions. As she herself recounted:

'At a recent lobster festival, the man on the mike looked up, saw me and said: "Welcome, Betty Hill! You've put us on the map with the greatest landing area for UFOs in the world!"'

Cynically, one could say that she developed a vested interest in having people believe that her experience was genuine, but there seems little question that she was completely sincere in her belief that the abduction really took place.

She also became no less convinced that a great number of strange events happened to her following the alleged abduction.

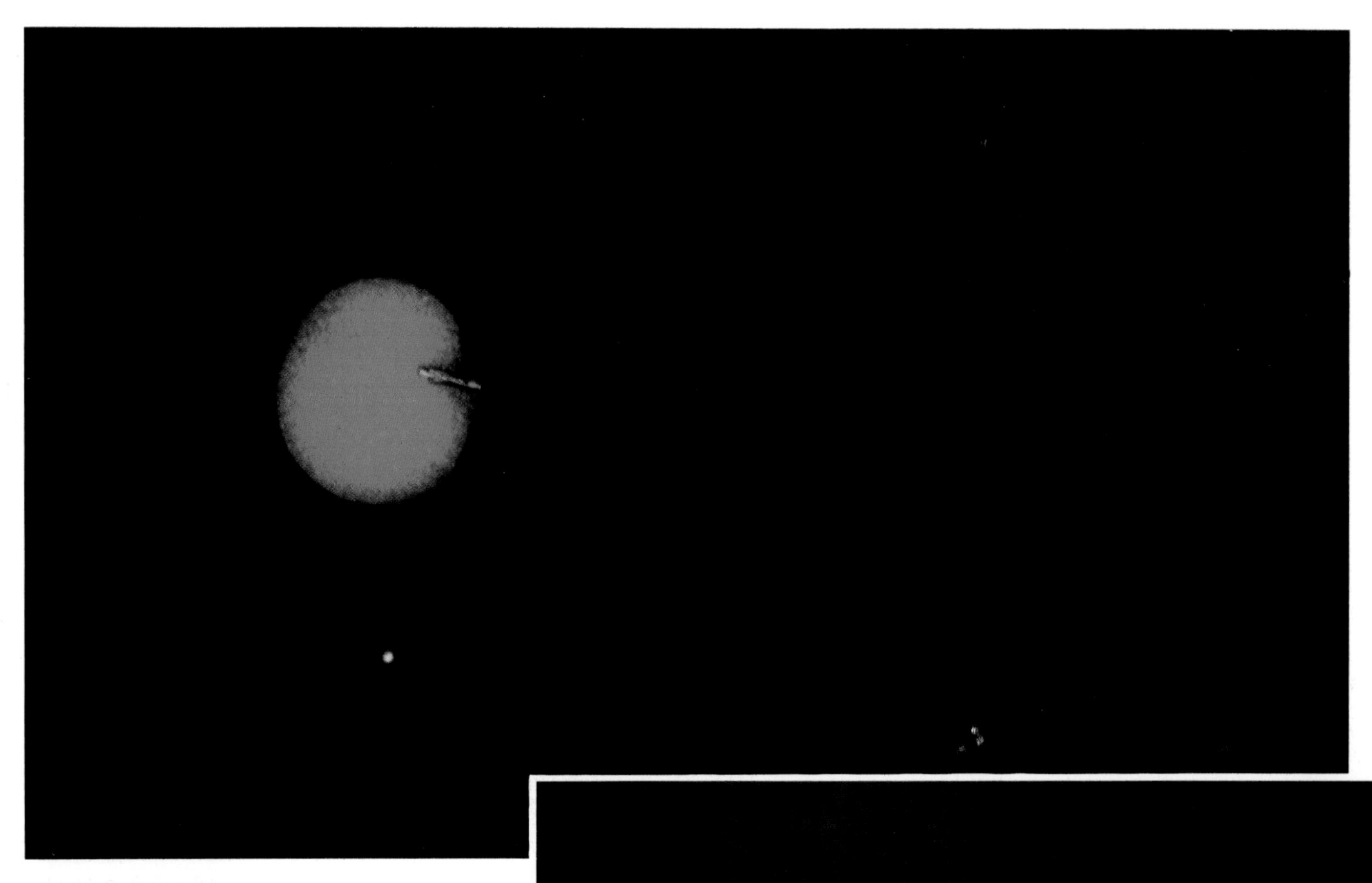

THE UNENDED JOURNEY

THE MOST FAMOUS OF UFO CLOSE ENCOUNTERS, THE ALLEGED ABDUCTION OF BETTY AND BARNEY HILL, CONTINUED FOR LONG AFTERWARDS. HERE, WE DESCRIBE THE SUBSEQUENT EXTRAORDINARY EXPERIENCES IN WHICH BETTY WAS INVOLVED

Not long after her UFO encounter, Betty Hill came home to find leaves piled inexplicably on her kitchen table. Among them were the ear-rings she had been wearing at the time of the sighting. Stranger and stranger incidents then occurred over the years. There were unaccountable noises around the house, and remarkable things happened to appliances: wires were pulled out of a central heating pump; a burglar alarm tripped off inexplicably; and faults developed in electrical equipment such as the refrigerator, toaster, iron, radio set and television, which just as strangely managed to right themselves. Betty finally claimed that her telephone had been tapped both by the Air Force and by some organization calling itself the 'Federal Agency'. Her mail disappeared; she saw and heard prowlers; and she was visited by all kinds of strangers.

While, for some of this, there is external confirmation – neighbours did indeed see prowlers round

PERSPECTIVES

NAZI ALIENS

At many points in the transcript of his hypnotic sessions, the latent fears of Barney Hill, *right*, come to the surface. While recalling watching the light in the sky, he says: 'Betty! This is not a flying saucer. What are you doing this for? You want to believe in this thing, and I don't.' When the object is close enough to appear like 'a big pancake, with rows of windows', he says: 'Can't somebody come and tell me this is not there?' One of the men on board apparently looked friendly, but another figure had an evil face: 'He looks like a German Nazi. He's a Nazi... '

Not surprisingly, considering he was black, Barney was terrified: 'His eyes! His eyes! I've never seen eyes like that before.' But after the experience, when he drove homeward, his former attitude returned. Betty asked him if he believed in flying saucers now, and he replied: 'Oh, Betty, don't be ridiculous.'

A huge red ball, filmed coming straight down from the sky,* above left, *and a double cylinder travelling along a beam,* left *– these are Betty Hill's descriptions of the objects that she filmed with a Super 8 movie camera in New Hampshire, not far from her home.

Betty Hill,* left, *reported frequent paranormal experiences and several sightings of UFOs each week. Sometimes investigators accompanied her, and reported that she misidentified aircraft and street lights. She believed, however, that she had found an actual UFO landing site in New Hampshire and that this accounted for the fact that she saw so many strange aerial objects.

Betty's home – most of it depends on Betty's own personal affirmation. However, in connection with another of her claims, she welcomed other witnesses: this was her UFO-hunting, which she went on to do several nights a week, whether with visitors or alone. She told the ufologist Allan Hendry that she often saw as many as 50 to 100 UFOs a night in a 'special area' in New Hampshire. In an interview, she told of one such incident:

'One particular UFO comes in almost every night. During the winter of 1976-1977, when I saw it often, it was quite spectacular – a sort of flattened disc with brightly coloured lights. One night in January 1977, it landed and turned on twelve big white lights around the rim. Under them, there were two white headlights. I was out there one night with a retired military officer and his wife. When he saw the UFO, he got out of the car and started walking towards it. Suddenly, a large swirling mass shot out from the object. I don't know what it was, but it looked like a red ball rolling over and over and heading directly toward him. I jumped out and tried to film this with my movie camera. But then – I know this sounds incredible – a green light hit my camera and burned out the switch and the circuitry so my camera wouldn't work. When the officer saw this red ball coming at him, he turned and ran back to the car. The red ball stopped, rolled back to the craft, and disappeared.'

But Hendry noted that 'a number of UFO field investigators have accompanied Mrs Hill to her special site, only to confirm that the lights in the night sky that Mrs Hill calls UFOs are only planes and street lights'; and he pointed out that 'she also related other tales involving robots, her neighbour's cat levitating, and a "militant" UFO that burned the paint on her car when she didn't leave the area soon enough to suit them.'

While it is fair to say that these bizarre incidents may be a consequence of her original experience, and do not therefore invalidate that experience, they cannot be dismissed as irrelevant. In a case that depends entirely on personal testimony, we must know just what kind of person is making the testimony. Psychology, not astronomy, may therefore best help us to understand the Hill case.

We should note that the Hills' story contains many incongruous or inconsistent features. It is not clear, for example, whether Betty is communicating with the aliens in speech or by telepathy: sometimes one is suggested, sometimes the other. In either case, the way the 'leader' used colloquial English is surprising in view of the ignorance the aliens displayed in some areas.

An example of seeming inconsistency is also afforded by the Hills' statement that, in being abducted, they walked – apparently, for some distance – through the woods with their abductors before reaching the clearing where the UFO was parked, whereas after the examination they were soon back at their car, from which they were able to watch the UFO's departure. Such details are not particularly important in themselves, but they serve to remind us that the Hills' story is by no means a precisely detailed and watertight narrative.

SOURCES OF STRESS

In the search for an explanation, the Hills' psychological history should be considered. Barney's health deteriorated during the year following the sighting, but it was by no means perfect before it. Barney did not develop an ulcer in 1962 – rather, the ulcer he already had grew worse. And an ulcer is notoriously the physical expression of psychological disturbance, usually stress. We have noted that both the Hills had been married previously and were separated from the children of those marriages; and, although their present marriage was, to all appearances, a happy one, it was none the less an inter-racial marriage in a society in which this was,

at the time, exceptional, and it remained a potential source of stress. Betty was employed in child welfare work, while Barney worked at nights, commuting 120 miles (200 kilometres) each day, and was involved in the civil rights movement: both these occupations were liable to produce anxiety.

Furthermore, Betty had a history of psychic experiences: she believed that psychic abilities were common in her family and said that she herself had traumatic precognitive dreams as a teenager. Curiously, this ability was also shared by her adopted daughter. 'Actually,' Betty told Dr Berthold Schwarz, a psychologist with an interest in UFOs, 'all my close family members have witnessed UFO sightings: my parents, my sisters and brothers, my nieces and nephews.' Poltergeist incidents of the type that occurred in the Hill household after the sighting had also been commonplace in her childhood home, where they were attributed to a 'ghost' named Hannah.

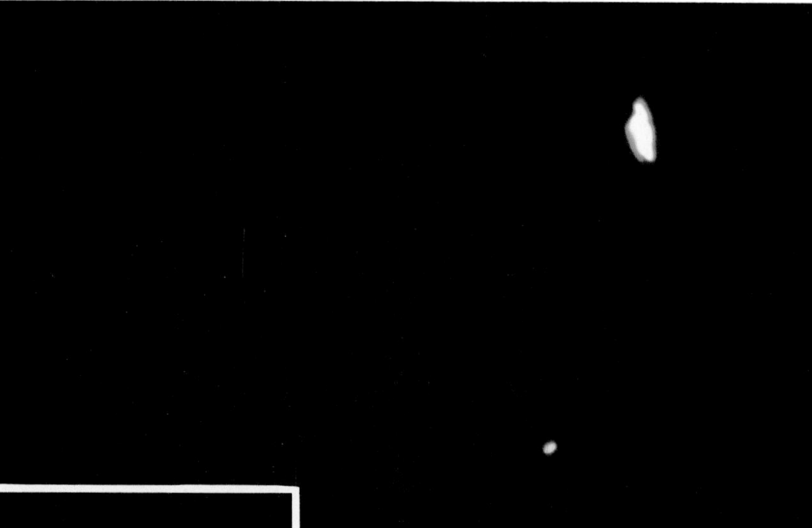

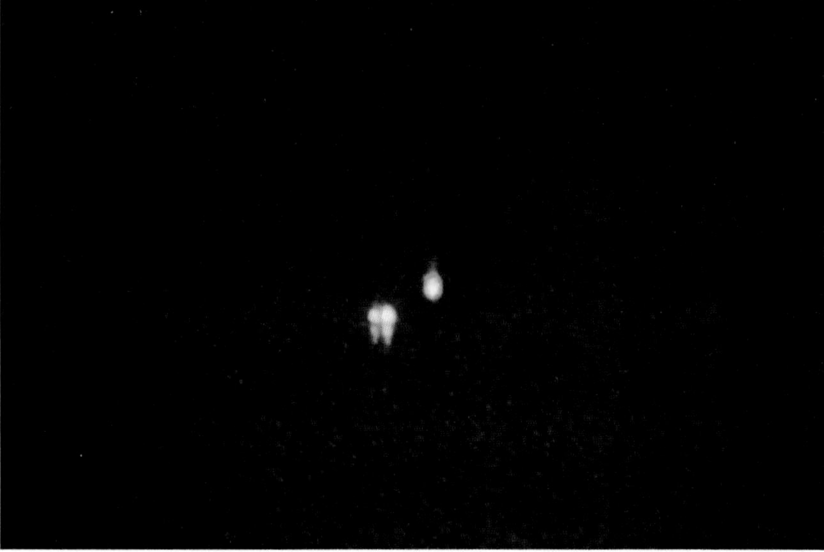

***Two more of Betty's UFOs, filmed near the coast, show a disc on edge with a small remote-controlled object under it,* top, *and three mushroom-shaped objects travelling together,* above.**

How does all this relate to their UFO sighting? Schwarz offers one possibility:

'In Betty's abduction case, as in some UFO contactee examples, there is the overall impression that the involved individual is a unique type of person, whose talents (such as the ability rapidly to enter a deep hypnotic trance, dissociative traits, and high-quality *psi* potentialities), latent or otherwise, are necessary for the UFOs, or the forces behind them... '

But Schwarz's view begs the question of whether any external agency was necessarily involved in Betty and Barney Hill's encounter. An alternative possibility is that there were no UFOs, nor any other external agency manifesting itself in that form, but that the whole experience was a 'projection' from an internal source, Betty's own mind. Many people have taken it for granted that Betty's dreams and the couple's hypnosis narratives are consistent with each other because both were derived from the same source – that is, an actual UFO encounter. But this, in many respects, is a naïve and unwarranted assumption – for it is no less possible that the stories recounted under hypnosis derive from Betty's dreams.

In fact, the moment we focus on Betty's dreams as a record of fact, the insubstantiality of the case becomes apparent. So what is the likelihood that Betty's dreams offer a reliable account of a factual experience? This is not what most dreams do; they are generally either total fantasy, or reworkings of material drawn from a whole variety of sources – the dreamer's daily life, books and television, wishes and fears. We must therefore be wary of supposing that Betty's dreams are any exception to this rule.

Dr Simon, the Hills' hypnotist, never committed himself to a definite statement, but put forward the possibility that Betty's recounting of her dreams had in turn influenced Barney, who then relived them as his own recollections of reality. It is noteworthy that, though Barney's UFO examination supposedly took longer than Betty's, his account of what was done to him during his experience is far less detailed than hers.

But why would Barney fantasize? He may, of course, have been looking for an external cause on which to blame his internal trouble, just as all of us are apt to do at times. The UFO sighting offered a convenient scapegoat. So Barney took Betty's fantasy and used it, albeit unconsciously, for his own purposes. But Dr Simon ruled out any question of conscious collusion, let alone deceit: whatever process was operating, it was completely on an unconscious level.

Dr Simon further warned that hypnosis is not a royal road to the discovery of truth, and further evidence has emerged in later years to confirm this. Hypnotic regressions, in particular, have been shown in numerous cases to produce narratives that are nothing more than fantasy. There is some evidence, on the other hand, for repressed experiences emerging as coherent, detailed and accurate narratives in dreams.

Inevitably, such an interpretation of the Hills' 'memories' of their abduction is bound to be pure conjecture. But it is not more conjectural than the hypothesis that the dreams and hypnosis stories recounted by Betty and Barney Hill are based on a real-life experience of a medical examination by beings from another world.

Could the UFO phenomenon be rooted in the traumatic experience of human birth, and is this a testable hypothesis?

ABDUCTIONS: THE INSIDE STORY

Red Indian shamans – Black Elk of the Oglala Sioux, for instance – believed that they could travel from Earth to other worlds via a 'cosmic pillar', often symbolised by a pole or a tree. Black Elk often chose a spot beside a tree to begin his trances. Shortly, a spirit guide in the form of a bird would lead him upwards through a tunnel-like aperture and then further upwards into a 'flaming rainbow tepee' where Black Elk met and communicated with a group of 'grandfathers'. At this point, in many accounts, the shaman would be forced to undergo painful bodily dismemberment – a demon supposedly removed every organ, bone and all the blood cells in his body. But everything would then be replaced, after being cleansed and purified, so that the shaman was spiritually and physically reborn, ready to return to his people with renewed spiritual energies. Sometimes Black Elk was returned on a 'little cloud'. 'Abduction' stories such as these, extraordinarily similar in many respects to UFO 'abduction' narratives with their echoes of the events that accompany birth, have been around for a very long time.

The American Indian medicine man, below, is seen entering a trance-state. Shamans – as recent as Black Elk of the Oglala Sioux, above – regularly underwent experiences somewhat similar to UFO abduction reports.

Those people who believe that UFO abductions relate to alien beings, parallel universes or other exotic origins will eventually have to explain – along with the lack of unambiguous physical evidence – why the incidents and images reported by abductees are so similar to those reported in a variety of obviously psychological processes, including drug-induced hallucinations, near-death experiences, religious and metaphysical ecstasies and, as we have seen, the trances of the shaman.

Every one of us has undergone a birth trauma. The universal phenomenon of birth is entirely free from ordinary cultural influences – for we experience it before we have undergone any kind of cultural conditioning – and it is, a far as we know, one of the first significant events consciously experienced by human beings. Although it is important to note that the causal link between specific events of biological birth and particular images has yet to be established, it seems that, in the birth trauma, we have a powerful experience that could well serve as the source of much imagery – including, perhaps, that reported by alleged victims of abductions by alien creatures. The fact that the experience of birth is more or less similar for everyone could indeed account for the similarity in abduction reports from all over the world; while the fact that no two births are absolutely identical could perhaps account for subtle differences.

When Betty Andreasson was abducted from her home in South Ashburnham, Massachusetts, on 25 January 1967, she found herself sitting in a clear plastic chair with a fitted cover filled with a grey liquid, as in the artist's impression,* left. *Closing her eyes, she felt pleasant vibrations and was fed sweet fluid through a tube in her mouth. The whole experience seems to be a classic reflection of good experiences in the womb.

> BETTY SPENT MUCH OF HER TIME ON BOARD THE UFO, FLOATING FROM ONE WOMBLIKE ROOM TO ANOTHER, THROUGH TUNNELS AND ON ELEVATORS OR OTHER COUNTER-PARTS OF THE BIRTH CANAL.

A classic abduction case can be used to illustrate this hypothesis. At about 7 p.m. on 25 January 1967, Betty Andreasson, of South Ashburnham, Massachusetts, USA, was allegedly abducted from her living room by a group of alien beings. Her abduction began with a bright light that flashed outside her house, shortly after which a group of 4-foot (1.2-metre) beings appeared. They communicated with Betty, and floated her outside into a waiting craft where she was examined, immersed in a liquid. She was apparently then taken for a journey into alien realms. At the climax of her adventure, she witnessed a huge bird that spoke to her and that then, phoenix-like, was consumed in flames – an event that Betty, a devout Christian, interpreted in religious terms. She heard a voice that she thought was God's, saying: 'I have chosen to show you the world,' seemingly because of her sincere faith. After this, Betty's captors returned her safely home. The alleged abduction had lasted about 3 hours and 40 minutes.

The Andreasson case is useful because it has been extensively investigated by a group of dedicated ufologists. The main witness is also considered reliable, and the case details are representative of abduction narratives as a whole. What is more, as a competent artist, Betty was able to provide many sketches of her adventure. In short, the Andreasson close encounter of the third kind is about as reliable and detailed as any abduction case we are likely to find. At the same time, it has significant implications for UFO abduction research, for it contains a wealth of images and events relating to birth that also support a non-physical or psychological interpretation of UFO abduction mysteries in general. For example, Betty's humanoids were of the classic foetal variety: they had greyish skin, oversized heads, huge eyes, and underdeveloped noses, ears and mouths, although they behaved much like apparitions in being able, it seems, to pass through solid doors and to materialise at will. The leader even seemed to change his facial features so that he became yet more foetal in appearance in his final meeting with Betty.

The event most obviously linked with perinatal imagery occurred in what Betty described as the cylindrical room, where she was enclosed in a clear plastic chair with a fitted cover, which her captors filled with a grey fluid. Here, she breathed through clear tubes that fitted into her nostrils and mouth. A telepathic voice then told her to close her eyes. Suddenly, she felt certain pleasing vibrations, the fluid whirled, and she was fed some sweet substance through the tube in her mouth. Floating and tranquil, she seemed to become one with the 'undulating fluid'. After a time, the fluid was drained, she was taken out, and she realised that her head hurt.

WOMB ANALOGIES

The cylindrical room is itself only one of several womb analogies in Betty's narrative: the transparent chair suggests the amniotic sac in which Betty floated in a foetal position; the grey liquid is the amniotic fluid; the breathing and feeding tubes are the umbilical cord. The tranquillising undulations and vibrations also suggest reference to 'good' womb experiences. Betty's headache may even be

The Garden of Delights *by Hieronymus Bosch,* below, *shows a kind of paradise and shares with many abduction cases the imagery of so-called 'good' womb experiences – a pleasant state of suspension within a transparent sac.*

Three Kentucky women, allegedly abducted by aliens, produced two sketches under hypnosis showing clear birth imagery. One depicts a woman on an observation table being examined by humanoids,* top, *a parallel with a baby's first moments. The other, a huge eye,* above, *is taken as a symbol of universal consciousness, often associated with tranquil periods within the womb.

a manifestation of the onset of another part of the remembered birth process – labour itself.

Betty spent much of her time on board the UFO, 'floating' from one womblike room to another, through tunnels and on elevators or other counterparts of the birth canal. The tunnels varied in length, but typically ended with doorways into brightly lit, dome-shaped rooms, where she was undressed, examined or 'cleansed'. The doorways suggest the cervical opening: usually a bare wall seemed to separate with a soft 'whoosh' on approach and unite again afterwards, leaving no trace. Other openings described include a circular membrane and mirror-like doors through which she crashed harmlessly.

During the medical examination that Betty alleges she underwent – in a big, bright room – the aliens inserted needle-tipped tubes into both her nasal cavities and her navel. In a hypnotic session conducted later by investigators, Betty recalled this experience in some detail as follows:

'I can feel them moving that thing . . . he's going to put it in my navel! O-h-h. I don't like this . . . I can feel them moving that thing around in my stomach or my body ... Oh! He's pushing that again . . . around, feeling things... Feels like he's going right around my stuff inside – feeling it, or something with that needle.'

Betty was informed by the aliens that the navel probe was a test for 'procreation', and afterwards was told that there were 'some parts missing'. Betty had indeed undergone a hysterectomy some time previously, and was evidently reliving her own medical history; but the navel also commonly appears as an analogue of the umbilical cord in abduction reports. The aliens said they were 'awakening' something with their probing – a reference, perhaps, to death and rebirth that was articulated, in Betty's case, more clearly by the phoenix.

In Betty's vision, a worm was seen to emerge from the ashes of the phoenix. At the same time, two things seemed to be happening to her, both relating in a way to well-established perinatal events: she felt an intense, shivering chill when only a moment before she had been complaining of intense heat, and also 'the worst thing I've ever experienced'.

It seems that the birth trauma hypothesis 'fits'. But is it correct to say that all abduction narratives are necessarily relivings of the subject's birth trauma? Even if this *is* the case, of course, it does not invalidate the experience nor in anyway prove that abduction experiences are all in the mind. What it does imply is that the UFO phenomenon may well stimulate a certain kind of hallucination in the human mind. The nature of the phenomenon itself, however, remains obscure.

PERSPECTIVES

SPIN-OFF CASES

As Robert Sheaffer recounts in his book *The UFO Verdict*, accounts of abduction experiences have been known to flood in following publicity given to any one case. In particular, numerous reports were made following the showing, on 20 October 1975, of a film dramatization of the well-known Hill abduction case that had occurred near New Hampshire's White Mountains.

Interestingly, some of these concerned sightings and missing hours that were only recognised as such following this dramatization, screened under the title *The UFO Incident*. In one case, involving Mrs Sandra Larson of Fargo, North Dakota, her daughter and a friend, all three underwent dissection, like frogs in a laboratory, but were then put back together again by the alien abductors – an experience remarkably similar to that of the Red Indian shaman, Black Elk, in his trances.

Certain subjects at first denied watching and therefore being influenced by the television dramatization, but subsequent questioning revealed otherwise. Indeed, details may have been unconsciously assimilated and worked into individual accounts, either genuine or fantasy, of experiences. A Defense Department memo, dated 11 November 1975, states: 'Since 28 October 1975, numerous reports of suspicious objects have been received at the NORAD COC' (Combat Operations Center). This was, of course, some eight days following the showing of the film.

THE CLOSEST ENCOUNTER EVER

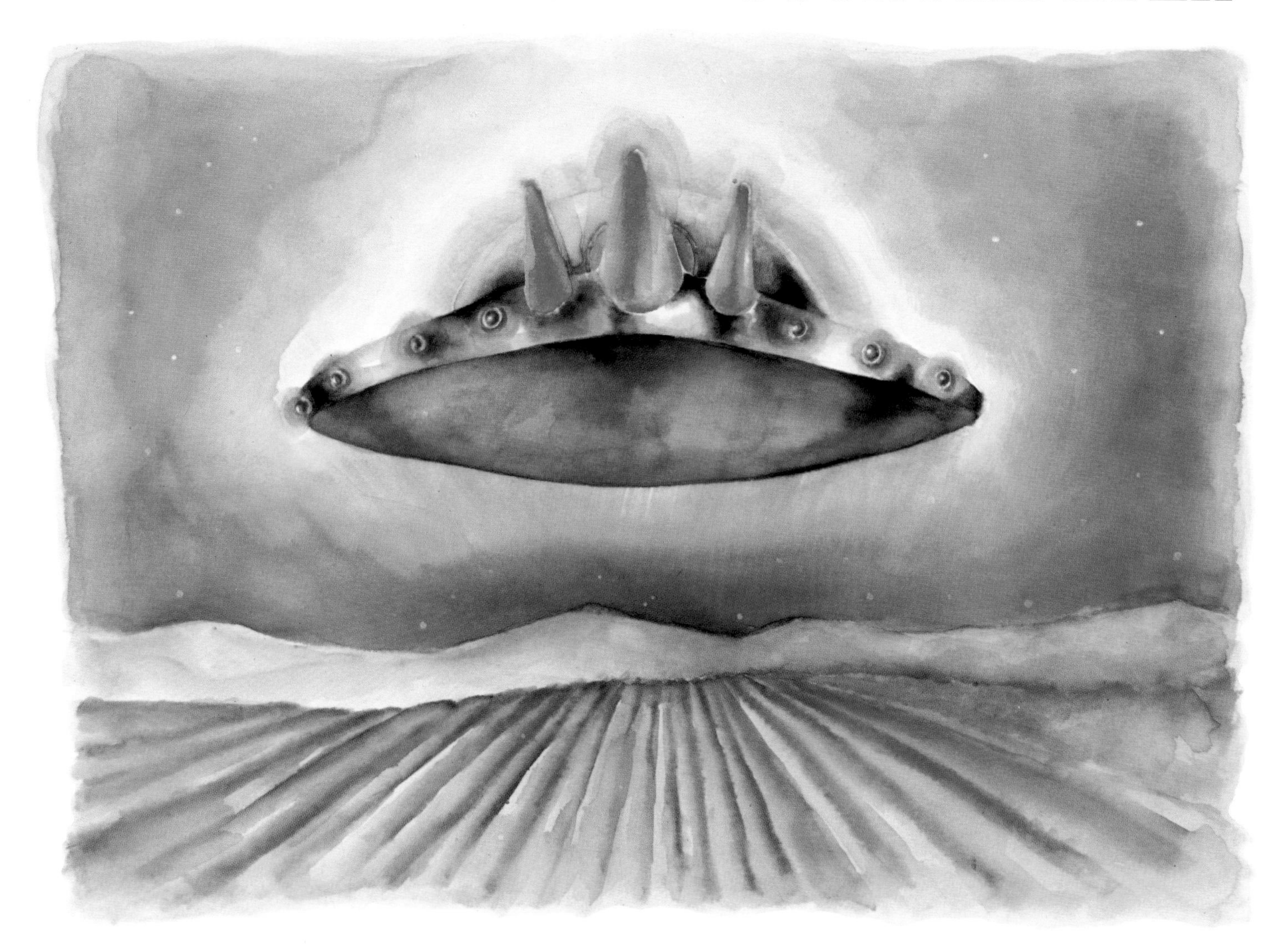

ONE OF THE PUZZLING FEATURES OF SO MANY UFO INCIDENTS IS THEIR APPARENT POINTLESSNESS. YET A BRAZILIAN FARMER WAS ALLEGEDLY ABDUCTED BY HUMANOIDS FOR A STARTLING PURPOSE: TO HAVE SEX WITH A BEING FROM ANOTHER PLANET

One of the earliest reports of an alleged abduction by humanoids was kept secret for over three years because it was deemed too 'wild' by those who first interviewed the abductee. This amazing case first became known when the victim, known only as A. V. B. to preserve his anonymity, wrote to João Martins, a Brazilian journalist, and his medical friend, Dr Olavo T. Fontes, towards the end of 1957. The man with the strange story was a young farmer who lived near the small town of São Francisco de Sales in Minas Gerais, Brazil. Intrigued, Martins and Fontes sent the farmer some financial aid so that he could make the long journey to the city of Rio de Janeiro, where the investigation began on 22 February 1958 in Dr Fontes' consulting room.

The story that unfolded was, the investigators felt, so astonishing that they decided to 'keep it on ice' in case a similar incident occurred that might corroborate any of the details. They also feared that if the account became widely known, there would be a rash of 'copycat' cases, which would end up invalidating the story. But a few details did leak out – fortunately in the right direction for the outline of the tale reached the ears of Dr Walter Buhler in 1961. As a result, he began to make his own detailed investigation.

The Buhler report eventually appeared as a newsletter and this, translated by Gordon Creighton and supplemented with editorial comments, appeared in *Flying Saucer Review,* in January 1965. Very soon after, João Martin's account was published in the Spanish language edition – not the Portuguese, as might have been expected – of the Brazilian magazine *O Cruzeiro*. Finally, the full case, including the results of various detailed clinical reports, was included in *The Humanoids,* a collection of accounts of encounters with UFO occupants, in 1969. At last, the story that had been thought too 'wild' to be made known to the public was in print and 'A.V.B.' was revealed to be 23-year-old Antônio Villas Boas.

Unidentified Lights

The actual abduction of Antônio Villas Boas was heralded by two unusual events. The first took place on 5 October 1957, when he and his brother were retiring to bed at about 11 p.m. after a party. From their bedroom window, they saw an unidentified light in the farmyard below. It moved up on to the roof of their house, and together they watched it shine through the slats of the shutters and the gaps in the tiles (there was no proper ceiling) before it departed.

The second strange incident occurred on 14 October at about 9.30 p.m. when the Villas Boas brothers were out ploughing with their tractor. They suddenly saw a dazzling light, 'big and round', about 100 yards (90 metres) above one end of the field. Antônio went over for a closer look, but – as if playing games with him – the light moved swiftly to the other end of the field, a manoeuvre it repeated two or three times. The young farmer tried to get a closer look at it. Then the light abruptly vanished.

The following night, 15 October, Antônio was out in the field again, ploughing alone by the light of his headlamps. Suddenly, at about 1a.m., he became aware of a 'large red star' that seemed to be descending towards the end of the field. As it came nearer, he saw that it was in fact a luminous egg-shaped object. The UFO's approach brought it right overhead, about 50 yards (45 metres) above the tractor. The whole field then became as bright as if it were broad daylight.

Villas Boas sat in his cab, transfixed with fear as the object landed about 45 feet (15 metres) in front of him. He saw a rounded object with a distinct rim that was apparently clustered with purple lights. A huge round headlamp on the side facing him seemed to be producing the 'daylight' effect. There was a revolving cupola on top, and, as he watched, fascinated, he saw three shafts – or 'legs' – emerge and reach for the ground. At this, the terrified farmer started to drive off but after a short distance, the engine stopped, despite the fact that it had been running smoothly. Villas Boas found he could not restart it and, in a panic, he leapt from the cab and set off across the heavily ploughed field.

Antônio Villas Boas, above, had a remarkable experience, at first concealed by UFO researchers because they considered it too wild to publish.

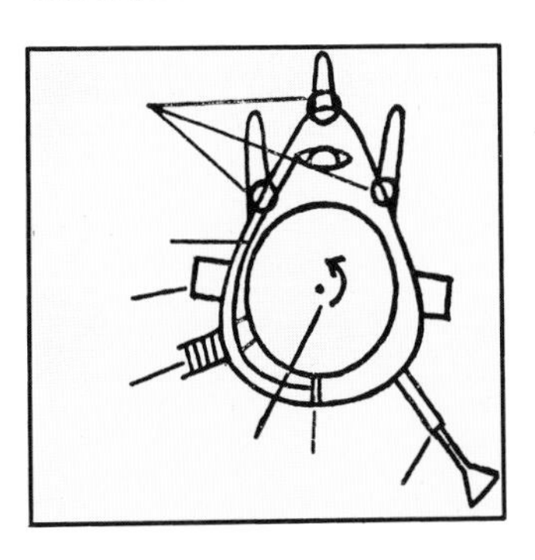

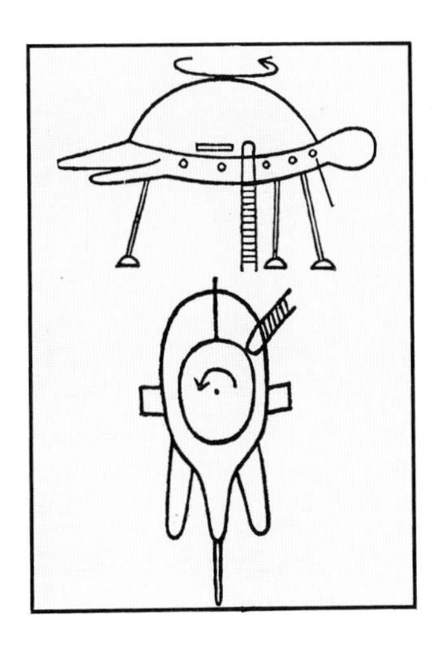

Sketches of the UFO were made by Villas Boas in February 1958 – above, for Dr Olavo Fontes, and in July 1961, below, for Drs Buhler and Aquino of the Brazilian Society for the Study of Flying Saucers.

Helmeted Aliens

The deep ruts proved a handicap to his escape and he had gone only a few paces when someone grabbed his arm. As he turned, he was astonished to see a strangely garbed individual whose helmeted head reached only to Villas Boas' shoulder. He hit out at the humanoid, who was knocked flying, but he was quickly grabbed by three other aliens who lifted him from the ground as he struggled and shouted. He later said, when revealing details about the extraordinary experience:

'I noticed that, as they were dragging me towards the machine, my speech seemed to arouse their surprise or curiosity, for they stopped and peered attentively at my face as I spoke, though without loosening their grip on me. This relieved me a little as to their intentions, but I still did not stop struggling'.

As he was carried to the craft, a ladder descended from a door, and his captors hoisted him up with great difficulty, especially as he tried to resist by hanging on to a kind of handrail. But, in the end, they succeeded.

Once inside the machine, Villas Boas found himself in a square room with metallic walls, brightly lit by small, high lamps. He was set down on his feet, and became aware that there were five small beings, two of whom held him firmly. One signalled that he should be taken through to an adjoining room, which was larger, and oval in shape, with a metal column that reached from floor to ceiling, together with a table and some swivel chairs set to one side.

A 'conversation' then ensued between his captors, who made sounds like dogs barking. As Villas Boas put it:

'Those sounds were totally different from anything I had heard until now. They were slow barks and yelps, neither very clear nor very hoarse, some longer, some shorter, at times containing several different sounds all at once, and at other times ending in a quaver. But they were simply sounds, animal barks, and nothing could be distinguished that could be taken as the sound of a syllable or word of a foreign language. Not a thing! To me it all sounded alike, so that I am unable to retain a word of it... I still shudder when I think of those sounds. I can't reproduce them... my voice just isn't made for that.'

Handled by Humanoids

This strange communication ceased abruptly, when all five set about him, stripping him of his clothing while he shouted and struggled – but to no avail. (Apparently they stopped to peer at him whenever he yelled; and, strangely, although they seemed to be using force, at no time did they hurt him.)

> " THE ALARMED VILLAS BOAS WATCHED THE CHALICE FILL WITH WHAT WAS PRESUMABLY HIS OWN BLOOD. THE CREATURES THEN LEFT HIM ALONE, CONTEMPLATING THE NIGHTMARE SITUATION. "

The beings were all dressed in tight-fitting grey overalls and large, broad helmets, reinforced at back and front with bands of metal. There were also apertures through which Villas Boas could see light-coloured eyes. Three tubes emerged from the top of each helmet, the central one running down the back and entering the clothing in line with the spine; the other two, curved away to enter the clothes, one beneath each armpit. The sleeves ended in thick gloves, which seemed stiff at the fingers. The trouser part fitted closely over seat, thighs and lower legs, and the footwear seemed an integral part of this section, the soles being very thick – about 2 inches (5 centimetres). On his chest,

The artist's impressions,* left *and* below, *show one of the humanoids seen by Villas Boas, and the inscription above a door in the humanoids' craft. In the statement he made to Dr Fontes, Villas Boas said it was a sort of luminous inscription – or something similar – traced out in red symbols which, owing to the effect of the light, seemed to stand out about 2 inches (5 centimetres) in front of the metal of the door. The naked female humanoid,* below right, *seduced Villas Boas aboard the craft.

each being had a kind of breastplate or 'shield', which was about the size of a slice of pineapple. It reflected light, and was joined to a belt at the waist by a strip of laminated metal.

The naked and shivering farmer – it was a chilly night outside, and no warmer in the craft – stood there quaking and 'worried to death'. He wondered what on earth was going to happen to him now. One of the little creatures approached him with what seemed to be a sort of wet sponge, which he rubbed all over Villas Boas' skin. As he later put it: 'The liquid was as clear as water, but quite thick, and without smell. I thought it was some sort of oil, but was wrong, for my skin did not become greasy or oily'.

He was now led to another door, which had an inscription in red over it. He tried to memorise this, although it meant nothing to him, since it was in unknown characters. In yet another room, one of the beings approached with a sort of chalice from which dangled two flexible tubes. One of these, with a capped end like a child's suction 'arrow', was fixed to his chin, while the other tube was pumped up and down. The alarmed Villas Boas watched the chalice fill with what was presumably his own blood. The creatures then left him alone, as he sat on a soft couch contemplating the nightmarish situation in which he found himself.

Suddenly, he smelt a strange odour, which made him feel sick. He examined the walls and saw metallic tubes at just below ceiling level. Grey smoke was coming through perforations in the tubes. Villas Boas rushed to a corner of the room and vomited, after which he felt a little less frightened. Moments later, there was a noise at the door, which opened to reveal a creature just like a woman. As Villas Boas gaped, the woman walked towards him. Flabbergasted, he suddenly realised she was naked, too.

The woman, said Villas Boas, was more beautiful than anyone he had met before. She was shorter than he, her head reaching only to his shoulder – he is 5 feet 5 inches (1.65 metres). Her hair was smooth, and very fair, almost white, and as though bleached. Parted in the centre, it reached halfway down her neck, with ends curling inwards. Her eyes were large, blue and elongated, 'slanted outwards'. Her small nose was straight, neither pointed nor turned up. She had high cheekbones, but – as Villas Boas discovered – they were soft and fleshy to the touch. Her face was wide, but narrowed to a markedly pointed chin. Her lips were thin, and her mouth like a slit. The ears were normal, but small.

The door then closed, and Villas Boas found himself alone with this woman, whose slim, lithe body was the most exquisite he had ever seen. She had high, well-separated breasts. Her waist was slender, her hips wide and her thighs large, while her feet were small and her hands, long and narrow. He saw, too, that the hair in her armpits, and her pubic hair, was a strange blood red. He smelt no perfume on her, 'apart from the feminine odour', which he noticed specifically.

> IF VILLAS BOAS' STORY IS TRUE, IT MAY WELL BE, THAT, SOMEWHERE OUT THERE IN THE UNIVERSE, THERE IS A STRANGE CHILD ... THAT MAYBE IS BEING PREPARED TO RETURN HERE.

She approached the farmer and rubbed her head against his (presumably by standing on tip-toe). Her body felt as though glued to his, and she made it quite clear what she wanted. His excitement welled up. The sexual act was normal – as was the one that followed – but then she tired, and refused further advances.

Villas Boas recalled that she never kissed him while they made love, nor were caresses exchanged, but she once gently bit him on his chin. Although she never spoke, she grunted, and that 'nearly spoiled everything, giving the disagreeable impression that I was with an animal'.

When she was called away by one of the other beings, she turned to Villas Boas, pointed to her belly, and then to the sky. These gestures instilled a great fear in Antonio – a fear that was with him years after the event – for he interpreted them as meaning she would return to take him away. (Dr Fontes later calmed him by suggesting that she meant: 'I am going to bear our child, yours and mine, there on my home planet'. This led to speculation by the farmer that all they wanted was 'a good stallion' to improve their stock.) Then Villas Boas was told to get dressed, after which he says he was taken on a conducted tour round the craft. During this time, he tried to steal an instrument merely for a keepsake, only to be rebuffed, angrily, by one of the alien crew. Eventually, he was invited by the humanoids to go down the ladder, and back on to solid ground. From there, he watched the ladder retract, while the metal legs and the lights began to glow. The craft rose into the air, its cupola turning at great speed. With lights now flashing, it listed slightly to one side, then suddenly shot off just like a bullet.

Villas Boas was examined by Dr Fontes, **below,** *in February 1958, four months after the alleged abduction. The symptoms he described suggested either radiation poisoning or exposure to radiation, but it was too late by this time for this diagnosis to be confirmed.*

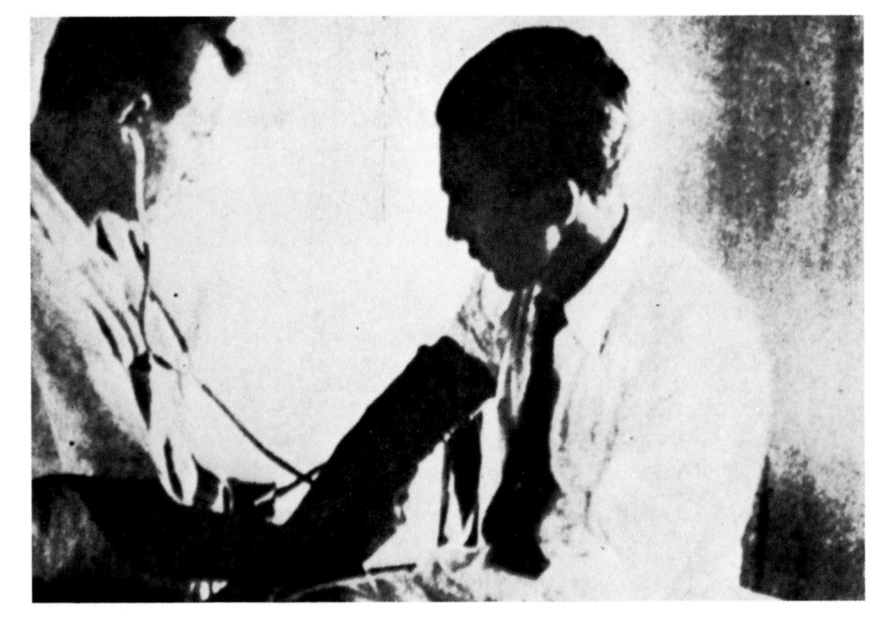

By now it was 5.30 a.m., so the abductee's extraordinary adventure must have lasted over four hours in all.

Villas Boas returned home, hungry and weakened by his spell of vomiting. He slept through to 4.30 p.m. and awoke feeling perfectly normal. But when he fell asleep again, he was restless, and woke up shouting after dreaming of the incident. Next day, he was troubled by dreadful nausea and a violent headache. When that left him, he found that his eyes began to burn. Unusual wounds, with infections, appeared on parts of his body; and when these dried up, he noticed that they left round, purplish scars.

Mysterious Scars

When Dr Fontes examined Villas Boas, he observed two small patches, one on each side of the chin. He described these as 'scars of some superficial lesion with associated subcutaneous haemorrhage'. Several other mysterious scars on his body were also noted.

In a letter to *Flying Saucer Review*, Dr Fontes suggested that the symptoms described pointed to radiation poisoning, or exposure to radiation. As he wrote: 'Unfortunately he came to me too late for the blood examinations that could have confirmed such a possibility beyond doubt'.

On 10 October 1971, João Martins was at last officially cleared to write about the case for the Brazilian public. His account eventually appeared in the Rio de Janeiro Sunday review *Domingo Illustrado.* An abridged account concluded with a fascinating statement confirming that:

'A.V.B. was subjected by us [Martins, Dr Fontes, and a military officer – whose presence was not revealed in the earlier reports] to the most sophisticated methods of interrogation, without falling into any contradictions. He resisted every trap we set to test whether he was seeking notoriety or money. A medical examination . . . revealed a state of completely normal physical and mental equilibrium. His reputation in the region where he lives was that of an honest, serious, hardworking man.'

Martins also revealed that the interrogation to which the abductee had been subjected at times bordered on harsh and cruel treatment, just short of physical violence, but Villas Boas never veered from his original story in any detail. The journalist therefore reached the rather intriguing conclusion that: 'If this story is true, it may well be that, somewhere out there in the Universe, there is a strange child ... that maybe is being prepared to return here.'

THE ALIEN THREAT

SOME UFOLOGISTS BELIEVE THAT THE POWERS BEHIND THE UFO PHENOMENON INTEND TO TAKE OVER MEN'S MINDS AND TURN US INTO A RACE OF ROBOT-SLAVES. WHAT EVIDENCE IS THERE FOR SUCH A CLAIM?

'Could I really be sure the people I was then talking with were representatives of the real space brotherhood who wished humankind well?' This was the dilemma facing Howard Menger, who in 1956 allegedly met a group of 'space people' who not only introduced him to space music and the space potato (with five times as much protein as the Earth-grown variety) but also revealed that he himself was Venusian, as was his second wife. The brotherhood claimed variously that they came from Venus, Mars, Jupiter and Saturn – and, as though that were not sufficiently confusing, they also announced that there were bad spacepersons as well as good. But since the bad ones always pretended to be good, how could a mere Earthling know whom to trust? Howard Menger takes up his story:

Howard Menger,* above, *was informed that he was a Venusian in an encounter with space people in 1956.

***Many people believe that UFOS presage Armageddon, as depicted in* The Great Day of his Wrath, *by John Martin,* below.**

'The man looked at me sadly. "My friend, this Earth is the battlefield of Armageddon and the battle is for men's minds and souls. Prayer, good thoughts and caution are your best insulation." I shouldn't have doubted these people for a moment, but I was quite ill at ease. I had been sheltered from the knowledge that all of the space people's work on this planet is not sweetness and light. The others I had contacted must have been on the "right side", for what I had seen convinced me they were a good people. Then the young lady spoke: "You don't know, Howard, that there is a very powerful group on this planet, which possesses tremendous knowledge of technology, psychology, and most unfortunate of all, advanced brain therapy. They are using certain key people in the governments of your world. This group is anti-God, and might be termed instruments of your mythical Satan. They are using the credulity and simple faith of many people to attain their own ends". There was both anger and frustration in her voice.'

The gathering swarms of UFOs have been taken as an indication of approaching crisis. Eric Norman, in his *Gods, Demons and UFOs,* cites the opinion of

The photograph taken by Howard Menger,* left, *is of an alleged space woman with a shining 'gadget' on her belt. The space woman gave Menger an explicit warning that a powerful group on Earth was using advanced brain therapy techniques to further the aims of Satan.

an unnamed research physicist at Stanford Research Institute, California:

'The mounting evidence leads me to believe that UFOs are extraterrestrial in origin, piloted by intelligent beings. Their appearance in recent years is probably in some way associated with the imminent second coming of Jesus Christ.'

Final Battle

Many Christians believe in the imminence of such a second coming; but traditional teachings are clear that Satan is not going to let Christ walk in and take over the Earth without putting up a fight. The belief in a 'final battle' is a key element in every scenario for 'the last days'. What is more, some say it is going to be a real war, fought by real people with real weapons. Dr Clifford Wilson, of New Zealand, has no doubt that the battle of Armageddon is scheduled for the very near future, and points out that satanic forces will need every single person who can be pressed into service. Consequently, he suggests, men and women are being brainwashed, even possessed, 'so that when the signal is given, they will be ready to give total allegiance to these beings who will then show themselves as their masters.

'Even the act of taking over humans is to be taken literally. It seems that when these beings enter the solid state which is necessary for humans to observe them, they utilise atoms from the world in which we live. They do actually take blood and other physical matter from human beings and animals alike. In this way, they are able to adapt themselves so that we limited human beings will understand them, and ultimately be programmed by them.'

The French theorist Jean Robin has taken a more subtle view. For him, UFOs are only the latest manifestation in a long tradition of strange reports; and what strikes him most forcibly about them is that they seem to be imitating – or perhaps mocking – human ideas. In 1886, he points out, Jules Verne wrote *Robur le Conquerant* which features a massive airborne 'clipper of the clouds'; a decade later, in America, there was a wave of UFO sightings in the form of airships, which at that date were purely experimental and seen only over France.

The subtitle of Robin's book is *The Great Parody*, and interestingly, every manifestation of the UFO phenomenon – the American airships of the 1880s, the Scandinavian 'mystery planes' of the 1930s, the Swedish rockets of 1946, the UFOs of today's space age – has been just one step ahead of human achievement. 'The heart of the problem,' he has insisted, 'is the projection of a false belief system, just beyond existing beliefs'.

So what is the point of this exercise? For some, it is a sign that the millennium is at hand, the advent of the brave new world brought by a new Messiah. But Jean Robin is less optimistic. According to him, we are in for 'a cursed time when there will reign beings who are almost totally dehumanised, robots or golems artificially and temporarily animated by the satanic spirit'. And, he adds, 'while it is certainly not our intention to forecast the precise form which the reign of the Antichrist will take, it is not too far-fetched to imagine him descending from a flying saucer'.

French theorist Jean Robin has suggested that the 'mystery planes' seen over Sweden during the 1930s,* below, *were an early manifestation of the UFO phenomenon. He noted that it seems to stay always one step ahead of Man's technological achievement. The aim, he believes, is 'the projection of a false belief system, just beyond existing beliefs'.

CASEBOOK

THE FISHERMEN'S TALE

The account of a close encounter that follows is one of the classics of UFO literature – and deservedly so, if the story told by the witnesses is true. But is it? The case is typical of many UFO reports: there were few witnesses, the bulk of the information coming from one man, as the second witness lost consciousness at the beginning of the incident. In such circumstances, even when sophisticated techniques, such as lie detector tests, are used, only the personal integrity of the witnesses can substantiate their story.

The six-month period from October 1973 to March 1974 was a remarkable one for UFO sightings, particularly in the United States, north-west Europe, Italy and Spain. One of the most outstanding reports in the USA came from Pascagoula, county town of Jackson County, in the state of Mississippi. This town, with a population of just under 30,000 at the time, is situated at the south of the Pascagoula River on the coast of the Gulf of Mexico, about 100 miles (160 kilometres) to the east of New Orleans.

There were two witnesses, both of whom worked locally at the Walker Shipyard: Charles E. Hickson aged 45, a foreman, and Calvin R. Parker Jr, 18, who alleged that, on 11 October 1973, they experienced a close encounter with a UFO and its occupants, and subsequent abduction, while fishing from the pier of the Shaupeter shipyard on the Pascagoula River.

It was about 9 p.m. when Hickson turned to get fresh bait. He says it was then that he heard a 'zipping' noise. Looking up, he saw an elongated, oval, bluish-grey craft, which in a later interview he was to refer to as 'a spacecraft'. It had very bright, flashing, 'blue-looking' lights. This object was hovering some 2 feet (60 centimetres) off the ground; and when the next move came, the witness was a trifle puzzled, for he said: 'It seemed to open up, but really there wasn't a door there at all . . . and three creatures came *floating out* towards us. I was so scared, I couldn't believe it was happening'.

The creatures were said to be pale, 'ghost-like', and about 5 feet (1.5 metres) tall. Their skin seemed to be wrinkled, and was a greyish colour, while in place of hands they had 'crab-like claws' or pincers. According to the witness's first report, these entities may have had slits for eyes, but he did not see them. They did have two small cone-shaped ears and a small pointed nose, with a hole below in the place of a mouth. They approached the two flabbergasted fishermen and floated just off the ground without moving their legs. A buzzing noise was heard from one of them and, said Hickson, 'they were on us before we knew it'. The older man was paralysed with fear, and Parker passed out when, apparently, he was touched by one of the creatures.

Meanwhile, two of the entities lifted Hickson from the ground, and they glided motionless into the craft. Hickson claims he had lost all sensation of feeling and weight. He was taken into a very brightly lit room which, however, had no visible light fixtures. His friend was led into another room by the

The artist's impressions show the spacecraft and its strange occupants that appeared in Pascagoula, Mississippi, in October 1973.

third entity. Hickson says he was placed in a reclining position and suspended in such a way that he did not touch any part of the craft. His limbs were completely paralysed; only his eyes were free to move. An instrument that looked like a big eye floated freely backwards and forwards about 9 inches (25 centimetres) above his body, and the creatures turned him so that all parts of his body came under the instrument's scrutiny. After some time, Hickson was guided back outside the craft and was 'floated', together with Parker, back to his position on the pier, landing upright on his feet. He says he was so weak-kneed that he fell over.

Calvin Parker was unconscious throughout the incident, so all the evidence comes from Charlie Hickson. In his first interview, he said the UFO was about 10 feet (3 metres) wide, and something like 8 feet (2.5 metres) high. When it left, he said, it disappeared from sight in less than a second. The occupants were like robots; they 'acted like they had a specific thing to do, and they did it. They didn't try to communicate with us.... I know now that they didn't intend to hurt us physically, but I feared they were going to take us away. I would like to emphasise that they didn't mean us any harm'.

Calvin Parker*, below, *was 18 years old at the time of the close encounter at Pascagoula. He apparently fainted when one of the humanoids touched him and remained unconscious throughout the incident. It was reported that he later suffered a nervous breakdown.

That statement was made in an interview with the *Mississippi Press* a week after the incident. On the day of the encounter, Hickson and Parker had called at the paper's offices, and found them closed. They then went to the sheriff's office, at 11 p.m., to make a report. Richard W. Heiden gave details of what took place in a report to *Flying Saucer Review.* Sheriff Fred Diamond and Captain Glen Ryder interrogated the witnesses, doing everything they could to break the stories, but to no avail. Ryder commented: 'If they were lying to me, they should be in Hollywood'. The interviews were taped. Then the two officers left the witnesses alone and unaware that the recorder was still running. They spoke agitatedly about their experience, and Calvin Parker was so emotionally overcome that he started praying when Hickson left the room. The sheriff was convinced the two fishermen were telling the truth.

THE OCCUPANTS WERE LIKE ROBOTS. THEY ACTED LIKE THEY HAD A SPECIFIC THING TO DO, AND THEY DID IT.

Next morning – Friday 12 October – detective Tom Huntley from the sheriff's office drove Hickson and Parker to Keesler Air Force Base at Biloxi, Mississippi, where they were checked for radiation. There was no evidence of contamination. While there, they gave details of their experience to the head of intelligence at the base, who 'acted as though he'd heard it all before!'

On Sunday, 14 October, the witnesses were interviewed by Dr J. Allen Hynek of Northwestern University, Evanston, Illinois, former civil scientific consultant on UFO reports to the US Air Force, and Dr James Harder of the University of California, Berkeley. Dr Harder hypnotised the men individually, regressing them to the time of the experience. They each relived the terror of the occasion to such an extent that Dr Harder said: 'The experience they underwent was indeed a real one. A very strong feeling of terror is practically impossible to fake

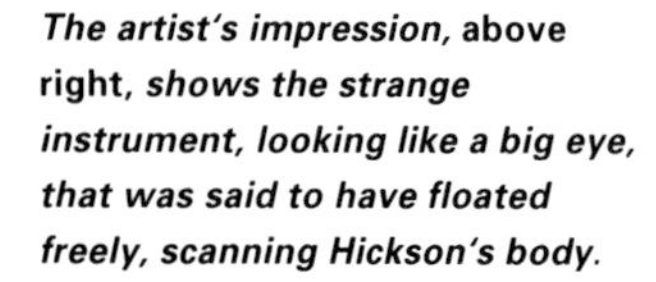

The artist's impression,* above right, *shows the strange instrument, looking like a big eye, that was said to have floated freely, scanning Hickson's body.

Charlie Hickson,* right, *was the principal witness at the scene of the Pascagoula incident. But doubt was cast upon his reliability since details of his story varied substantially with each retelling.

severe eye injury, which had persisted for about three days.

These discrepancies, of course, tend to cast doubt upon the entire story – although they do not disprove it. But there are reports that possibly corroborate the evidence. Although no one but Hickson and Parker saw the UFO – despite the fact that the incident happened close to Highway 90, a busy road – many owners of television sets in the Pascagoula area reported interference.

On the same day, 11 October, 450 miles (700 kilometres) away near Hartwell, Georgia, a former Methodist minister was driving along when he saw a UFO land on the road in front of him. He also saw silver-suited, white-haired occupants.

On the same night, too, Police Chief Greenhaw of Falkville, Alabama, was telephoned by a woman who claimed that a 'spaceship' had landed in a field near her house. He raced to the location, armed with a Polaroid camera. There was nothing at the alleged site, but Greenhaw said he was confronted by a silver-suited creature on a side road. He took four Polaroid shots – which indeed show a silvery creature, obligingly turning to face the camera. The entity bolted, and Greenhaw gave chase in his patrol car, but failed to catch up with it – an inconclusive end to an intriguing series of events.

Dr James Harder,* above left, *and Dr J. Allen Hynek,* above right, *interviewed Charlie Hickson and Calvin Parker shortly after their alleged abduction. Dr Harder hypnotically regressed the men to the time of their experience and both scientists later agreed that the witnesses had been subjected to some very terrifying experience – although they were unable to say precisely what it involved.

under hypnosis'. Dr Hynek was more reserved: 'There is no question in my mind that these men have had a very terrifying experience'.

On 30 October, Hickson – but not Parker who was apparently suffering from a nervous breakdown – underwent a polygraph examination (lie detector test) at the Pendleton Detective Agency in New Orleans. It was reported that the polygraph operator, Scott Glasgow, was forced to admit after 2½ hours of exhaustive tests that Hickson was telling the truth.

If this is true, it was a very strange remark for a polygraph operator to make. Polygraph tests are not sufficient to establish that a subject is lying; and any polygraph operator would have been well aware of this. In his book *UFOs Explained,* Philip J. Klass claims that his own investigations have shown that Scott Glasgow was not, in fact, qualified as a polygraph operator. So it seems that, in spite of the newspaper publicity given to the fact that Hickson's story stood up to the lie detector test, it must remain inconclusive.

Hickson's experiences brought him considerable publicity; he appeared on television shows and even wrote a book. But unfortunately, his story often changed in the telling. Originally, for instance, he claimed that the UFO was some 10 feet (3 metres) long; but in subsequent interviews, he said it was 20 or 30 feet (7 or 10 metres) long – quite a difference.

Hickson's descriptions of the alien creatures also varied on different occasions. In his original account, Hickson claimed they had two small, cone-like ears, possibly slits where the eyes should have been, and a small sharp nose with a hole below it. Later, again on a television show, he said there were no eyes and that the hole below the nose was a slit. And more than a month after the incident, he disclosed for the first time that the light inside the spacecraft had been so bright that he had suffered

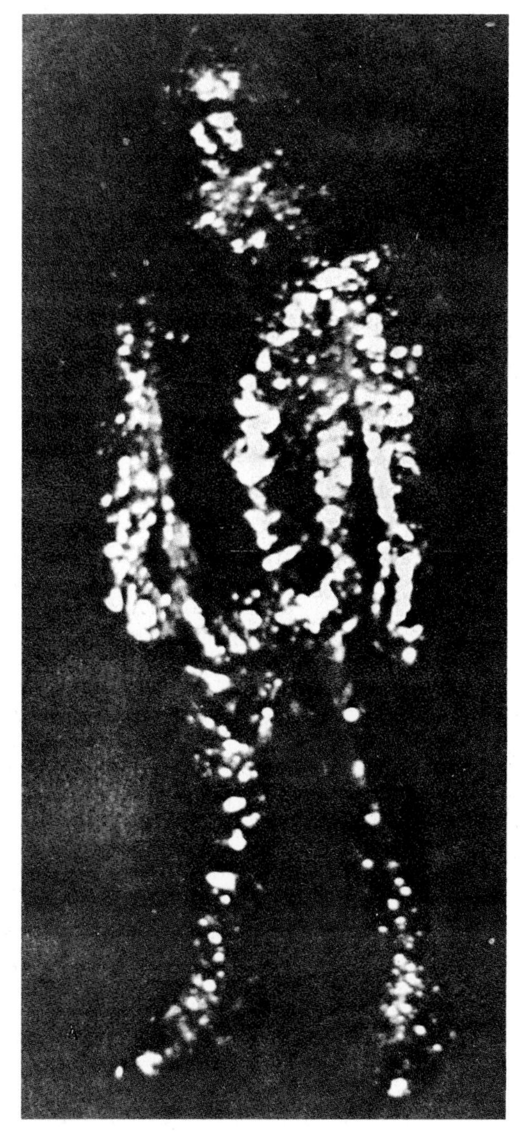

The 'UFO entity',* right, *was photographed with a Polaroid camera by Police Chief Jeff Greenhaw at Falkville, Alabama, on the night of the Pascagoula encounter. The entity reportedly bolted. Greenhaw drove after it in his patrol car, but did not succeed in catching it.

THE GOOD, THE BAD AND THE UGLY

THE CREATURES DESCRIBED IN CLOSE ENCOUNTER REPORTS COME IN A CONFUSING VARIETY OF SHAPES AND SIZES. WHAT ARE WE TO MAKE OF THEM?

The classic picture of an alien being is of a small, spindly creature with a large head and bulbous eyes, but often no other visible facial features, dressed in a one-piece grey suit that seems to be without buttons or zips. The startling similarity of descriptions of aliens in many close encounter reports has led to speculation that all UFOs probably originate in one place. But for every report of foetus-like aliens, there is one of creatures of a completely different kind, sometimes stiffly moving, like robots, sometimes indistinguishable from human beings, sometimes green and gnome-like.

What can ufology make of this fascinating but bewildering array of descriptions of supposed alien life forms? Are we to suppose that planet Earth is being bombarded with spacecraft from many alien cultures, all conducting reconnaissance missions, and that pilots of the alien craft have some obscure purpose in disguising themselves now in one form, now in another? Or will we be forced to make a more radical hypothesis?

A good starting point is the creating of a tool for analysing the wealth of reports of close encounters of the third kind – those UFO reports that involve aliens. For this, some kind of classification system will be useful, starting with those aliens that take the same basic form as human beings, and that are immediately identified as such by the witnesses. They are generally dressed in one-piece suits, and move and speak normally. Their average height, in all the reports, is between 5 and 7 feet (1.5 – 2.1 metres). Humanoids, meanwhile – perhaps the most commonly reported aliens – resemble humans, but witnesses report clear anatomical differences. They often have disproportionately large heads, pallid skins, underdeveloped facial features, and hairless bodies – giving them an appearance reminiscent of human foetuses. The single feature most often reported is their exceptionally large eyes, sometimes described as unblinking, or with vertical pupils. They are small, with an average height of between 3 and 5½ feet (90 centimetres – 1.7 metres). Unlike human entities, they generally communicate not through normal speech, but telepathically; but like them, humanoid entities are generally dressed in one-piece, close-fitting suits, usually of silver or grey, although space-suits are also sometimes reported.

Somewhat rarer are 'animal entities'. These are characterised by distinctly mammalian, reptilian, fishlike or other features, including fur, claws, a tail, scales or other strange skin texture, pointed ears, a snout, enlarged teeth, and non-human eyes. Their heights range from 6 to 8 feet (1.8 – 2.4 metres). Most are ape-like in appearance, and walk on two legs. Their method of communication ranges from animal cries to telepathy.

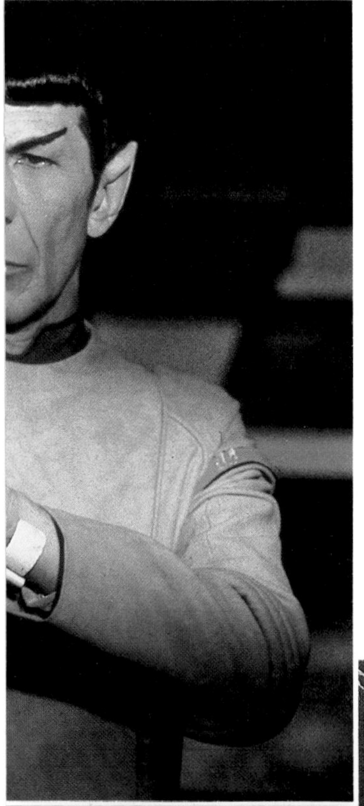

Alvin Lawson has proposed a sixfold classification of alien beings as reported in close encounter cases. Mr Spock,* above left, *from television's* Star Trek, *is an example of the 'human entity' category. In an illustration from a 1918 issue of the French magazine* La Baionnette, left, *lunar entities – evidently belonging to Lawson's humanoid class – conjecture that Earth wars are a device to prevent the planet cooling. The Cyclops of Greek legend,* far left *– in a painting by Odilon Redon – is a member of Lawson's 'exotic' class; and the Greek river god Achelous,* above *– seen here with Herakles – is an example of an apparitional entity – with the ability to change his shape at will.

Another form of alien is the 'robot entity'. Robots seem to be made of metallic or other artificial body materials, and often move in a jerky, stiff or otherwise unnatural manner. Glowing eyes are often reported, as is the robots' ability to float, or to cause witnesses to float. Their shape varies from bipedal to huge machines; and their height can be anything between 6 inches and 20 feet (15 centimetres – 6 metres). They often wear padded spacesuits with bubble-dome headgear. Their method of communication varies from a flat metallic voice to telepathy.

Other types of alien exhibit a variety of strange characteristics – they are the 'exotic entities'. They may have grotesquely exaggerated animal or human features, and may combine human characteristics with non-animal ones – humans with robot arms, for instance. Most are bipeds; but some combine the characteristics of two or more of the other categories. They range in height from 1 to 10 feet (30 centimetres – 3 metres). They may move like humans or animals, or like robots, or even float; and they often communicate telepathically, rather than by what for us are more ordinary means.

A final category is also the most puzzling. It consists of 'apparitional entities' – aliens that share many of the characteristics of ghosts. They may materialise or dematerialise, change form, manifest themselves selectively to witnesses, or move matter, including people, at will. Their average height is 5 to 6 feet (1.5 – 1.8 metres); they often float rather than walk; and again, they generally communicate by telepathy. They also most often appear dressed in one-piece suits.

This system of classification can be used to analyse the close encounter cases described in Webb's *1973 – Year of the Humanoids*. Of a total of 66 cases, 16 were humanoids; 12, robots; 10, human; eight, animal; seven, exotic and five, apparitional – while eight were impossible to categorise because the descriptions were so vague.

Stranger Still

Some scientists have even gone so far as to speculate about the existence of alien creatures that are so unusual that it would be impossible to classify them under the six-category system already given. In his novel *The Black Cloud,* for example, astronomer Sir Fred Hoyle described a vast, intelligent cloud that 'lives' in interstellar space, complete with molecular heart system, brain and other necessary organs. It feeds on raw energy and its central nervous system functions via radio waves. Ronald Bracewell, in his book *The Galactic Club,* imagines an 'intelligent scum' – colonies of single-celled plants that could, with time, gain technological control of their environment. But, in fact, such creatures are rarely, if ever, encountered in genuine close encounter reports.

IS ANYBODY OUT THERE?

EVEN IF SOMEONE IS INDEED LISTENING, WILL OUR MESSAGES NECESSARILY BE UNDERSTOOD?

Mankind's first radio message to the stars was transmitted at 5 p.m. on 16 November 1974 by the world's largest radio telescope, a disc 1,000 feet (300 metres) in diameter, situated in Puerto Rico. The message was a three-minute signal sent out across the vastness of space towards a group of stars 24,000 light years away. It is believed to be the strongest signal yet radiated by mankind; and in the words of the Arecibo staff, it was intended to be 'a concrete demonstration that terrestrial radio astronomy had now reached a level of advance entirely adequate for interstellar radio communication over immense distances'.

The Arecibo transmission was a statement of faith by the scientific community. It bore witness to the confidence of scientists that intelligent extra-terrestrial beings exist and are 'out there' listening. In fact, many people would argue that it would be very surprising indeed if Man were alone in the galaxy in which he lives, and more surprising still if there were no other beings to share the huge Universe. It has even been suggested that there are millions of Earth-like planets among the billions of planets in the galaxy, and that the conditions essential to the emergence of life must have been present on such planets on innumerable occasions. If that is the case, it is likely not only that extra-terrestrial intelligence (ETI) exists, but also that in many cases the technology of civilisations of other planets must have developed to a stage as advanced as, or even much more advanced than our own.

From the Arecibo observatory in Puerto Rico, **above,** *astronomers sent out Earth's first radio message to a group of stars, 24,000 light years away. Microwave receiving dishes, such as the one,* **inset above,** *meanwhile, have for years been leaking signals into space.*

The impulse to attempt to make contact with beings on other planets is clearly very strong in Man. In the mid-19th century – a hundred years before sophisticated technology made such ambitions at all realistic – many people took it more or less for granted that there were civilisations on other planets that could be reached with the aid of science, and various methods of communicating with these civilisations were proposed.

The French inventor Charles Cros (1842-88), for example, suggested the construction of a vast mirror that could be used to reflect sunlight from Earth to Mars. It could be tilted, he thought, to flash out a form of code. (The idea was ingenious, but it raised an insurmountable problem: there was, of course, no guarantee that a Martian civilisation would recognise or be able to respond to such a code.)

Spectacular Messages

Nevertheless, interest in establishing communication with extra-terrestrial beings soon grew to fever pitch. In Paris, in 1900, for example, a prize of 100,000 francs was offered to the first person who would manage to make contact with ETI. The competition excluded communication with Mars, however – that was thought to be far too easy a feat to be worth the money!

These enthusiastic early experiments proved fruitless, however. It is doubtful whether the crude techniques that were suggested could have served the purpose of initiating contact with extra-terrestrial civilisations, and it has since been established that there is no ETI on the Moon, on Venus or on Mars. Yet the search for intelligent life on other planets continues; and, ironically enough, in the 20th century, we have transmitted spectacular messages to the stars with no special effort.

Since the 1940s, powerful microwave beams from radar and TV transmitters have been leaking out into space. This radio noise is already washing over the stars nearest to Earth like a tide of electromagnetic flotsam; and although its intensity is minute, a sufficiently sensitive receiver could pick up the signal as far as 40 light years away.

Meaningful Signals

So what would an extra-terrestrial astronomer make of this swelling tide of radio noise? If he had sustained his observations over a long period of time, he would have made an interesting discovery: today, Earth is emitting radiation at the frequency of radio waves that is a million times more intense than it was a few decades ago. And if he used his radio telescope to measure the radio power emerging from this small planet at metre wavelengths, he would make an even more astounding discovery: Earth is emitting almost as much radiation as the Sun at a time of low sunspot activity. In fact, in the radio spectrum, our planet is as bright as a star!

The tiny human outline in the picture, **right,** ***is an artist's impression of what an illuminated figure would look like from Mars. The shape – which was to be formed by illuminating 'several square miles' of snow with electric lamps – was proposed in 1893 as a means of communicating with other planets.***

Another late-Victorian proposal – a cross of powerful electric lights to be strung across Lake Michigan – is demonstrated **below.** ***The lights would flash on for 10 minutes and off for another 10 – an artificial phasing that, it was hoped, would attract interstellar attention.***

Hydroxyl and hydrogen, which together make water, **right,** ***could be widespread emitters of microwaves in space. Indeed, the wave band from 17-21 centimetres is sometimes called the 'waterhole'. The name is also apt because of the hope that different extra-terrestrial civilisations may send and receive messages in this band, just as different species come to drink at waterholes on Earth.***

Extra-terrestrial scientists would perhaps attempt to formulate a 'natural' explanation for the phenomenon; but any such attempt would eventually prove unsatisfactory. They would be forced to acknowledge that the radio emission could not be explained by the action of natural forces: it could only be produced by artificial means. However, scientists on other planets might not regard such weak signals as incontrovertible proof of the existence of a civilisation somewhere near our Sun. Even if they concluded that a civilisation did exist, they would probably find it impossible to make sense of the complicated mix of signals.

One solution to this dilemma is for us to indicate our presence unambiguously by transmitting a constant and deliberate message via a powerful radio beam, aimed at the stars. Existing radio telescopes provide us with the technological means to do this.

CLOSE ENCOUNTERS OF THE THIRD KIND

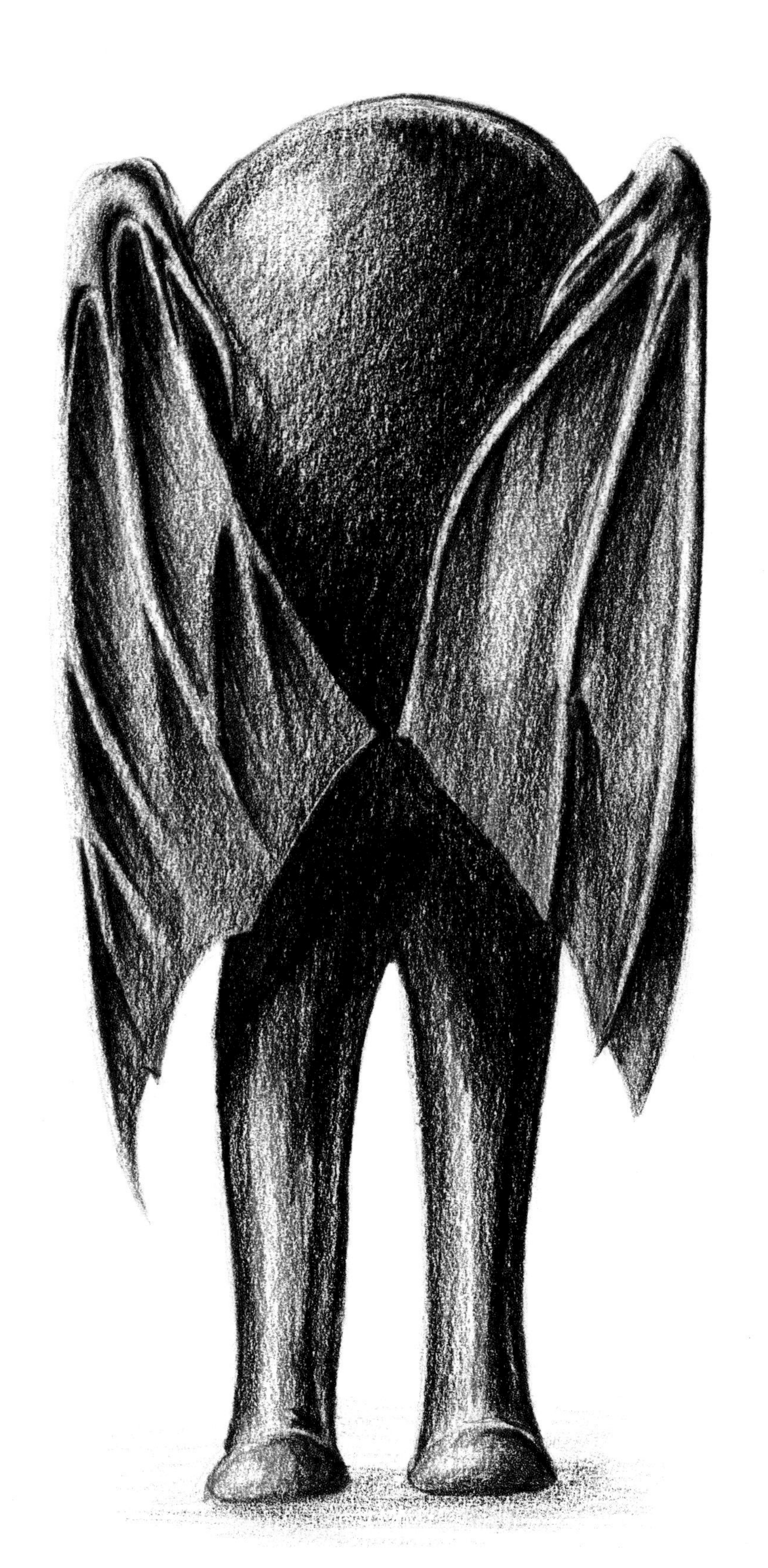

IS THE POSSIBILITY OF COMING FACE TO FACE WITH A HUMANOID OR OCCUPANT OF A UFO INCREASING? WHO OR WHAT ARE THESE CREATURES, AND HOW 'REAL' ARE THEY?

As more and more reports of UFO sightings were collected throughout the 1950s and 1960s, an interesting pattern soon became apparent in that there seemed to be a marked peaking of UFO activity. This came to be known as the 'wave' or 'flap' phenomenon and, invariably, at or around the crests of the waves came reports of humanoid occupants of the UFOs – a phenomenon within a phenomenon.

Perhaps the most intense flap of all, so far, was that of 1954 in north-west Europe, particularly France. Other great waves since then have included those of 1957-58 (in the Americas and Australasia), 1962-63 (in South America), 1964 (USA), 1965 (worldwide), and 1977-78 (Britain and Italy).

The 1954 wave was very complex, with one main and several secondary peaks: and then came reports of widespread humanoid encounters. The Quarouble case, of 10 September 1954, involved grotesque dwarves in diving suits and a craft with an immobilising beam. Shortly after that there was another report from France, near Cénon where, at 10.30 p.m. on 17 September 1954, a farmer on his bicycle suddenly started to itch all over. He dismounted and slowly became immobilised (he described it as being 'paralysed') as he observed a 'machine' on the road ahead of him. A little creature, apparently clad in a diving suit, came towards him, uttered strange sounds, and touched the farmer's shoulder before moving off to enter the object, which glowed green and took off like lightning. As it disappeared, the farmer found that he regained his mobility.

CREATURES OF TERROR

Next came an account with a hint of menace. At 8.30 p.m. on 27 September 1954, four French children, playing in their father's barn at Prémanon, high in the Jura Mountains, heard their dog barking. The eldest went to investigate and encountered a creature, described as being 'like a sugar lump' standing on end and split at the bottom. He threw pebbles and shot a toy arrow at it, and then moved as if to touch the thing, only to be flung to the ground by an invisible force. He screamed, jumped up and ran into the yard, where he saw the 'being' waddling towards a meadow.

The children then ran to the house and, on the way, saw a glowing red sphere wobbling over the meadow grass, 165 yards (150 metres) away. The next day, gendarmes discovered a 13 foot (4 metre) diameter circle of flattened grass there.

At 7 p.m. on 9 October 1954, a labourer cycling at Lavoux, near Poitiers in France, met a weird 4 foot (1.3 metre) tall creature, again apparently in a diver's suit. What could be seen of its head looked like a mass of hair with big eyes shining through. The creature shuffled along the road for a minute, and then disappeared into the adjacent trees.

Not surprisingly, this story became the subject of hilarious jokes in the French national press. What the journalists did not know, however, was that, on 10 October in north-eastern France at Pournoy-la-Chétive (in the Moselle area), at about 6.30 p.m., a 'shiny machine' was seen to land by three children who were out roller-skating. A 'kind of man', just under 4 feet (1.2 metres) tall, emerged dressed in a black sack, like a priest's cassock. They later described him as 'a ghost'. His face was very hairy and he had big eyes. He held a flashlight that dazzled the children, and uttered words they did not understand. Frightened, they beat a hasty retreat: then, looking back, they saw the machine climb rapidly into the sky.

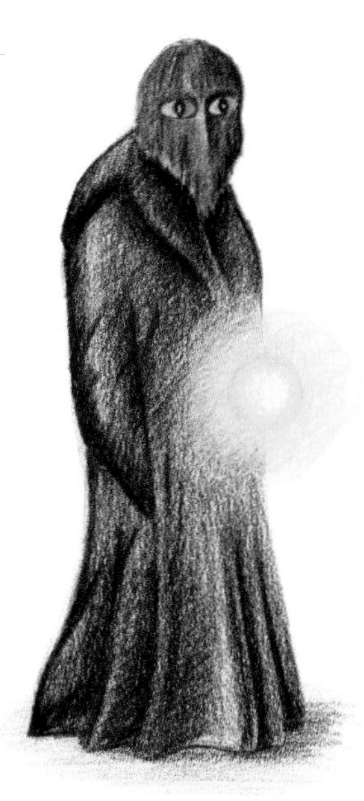

The artist's impression,* far left, *shows the black, headless creature that terrified a group of young people in Kent, England, in 1963.

Dressed in a cassock-like robe, with a mass of hair for a face and described as 'a ghost', the humanoid,* left, *was witnessed by three French children in 1954.

During an encounter in Finland in 1971, illustrated* below, *a forestry worker was burnt on touching what seemed to be a humanoid.

These were the only sightings. The following day, three men from Bordeaux were driving at Tapignac, on the Atlantic coast of France, when they saw a red glow lighting up the fields and sky – it was about 7.30 p.m. They stopped, got out, and saw a disc-shaped object with a red-orange dome about 275 yards (250 metres) away, hovering about 35 feet (10 metres) above the ground. After a few seconds, it moved away to the trees where its light was still visible. The men took a torch and walked towards the light when, some 450 yards (400 metres) away, they came upon the object, now landed and with four 3 foot (1 metre) tall 'beings' busy at some task under the craft. The creatures then disappeared inside the disc. After undergoing rapid colour changes, the object took off at great speed.

The diversity and variety of reported humanoid behaviour is immediately apparent, even from this small sample of case histories – entities who were tall, gawky and gambolling, wearing transparent suits; tall and well-shaped beings apparently dressed in cellophane; armless midgets, shuffling along in garb similar to divers' suits with massive helmets; waddling, rectangular creatures like sugar lumps who pack a hidden punch; hirsute, pop-eyed monsters in black, sack-like clothing. Also reported were entities tapping shoulders or brushing coldly past; and aliens hurling boulders, playing hide-and-seek, or seen tinkering beneath their craft.

Reliable Witnesses

But what of the eyewitnesses who experience such 'close encounters of the third kind'? (The phrase was first used by Dr J. Allen Hynek in his book *The UFO Experience*, and has since been borrowed spectacularly by film-makers.) They have included surveyors, prospectors, ranchers, businessmen, children, farmers, a labourer and a professor. If the doctors, police officers, servicemen, housewives, scientists, factory workers and airmen, all of whom have had a variety of similar experiences, and who help to make up a very fair cross-section of the public, are added to the list, strikingly consistent patterns of behaviour emerge.

The contactees are subsequently deeply disturbed, amazed or frightened, and feel an obsessive obligation to discuss the incident with friends, or are strongly motivated to report it to the authorities.

Very few of the thousands of witnesses of this kind actively seek publicity, go off on lecture tours, or write books about their encounters. Yet the very nature of the contact with humanoids, the strange dreamlike quality of many of the reports, and the inconclusiveness and pointlessness of many of the activities of the creatures seen – all militate in favour of the stories being accurate representations by the witnesses of what they saw. Hoaxers might well feel compelled to give their stories a neater shape and a definite message.

The flow of humanoid reports continues unabated. At about 3 p.m. on 5 February 1971, for instance, two forestry workers at Kinnula, Finland, saw a UFO that landed on stilt-like legs in the clearing where they were working. A creature that was less than 3 feet (1 metre) high, clad in a green one-piece suit, including a helmet equipped with a lens, emerged from an aperture in the craft and glided towards them. The creature's hands appeared rounded, and there were no fingers visible.

One worker went forwards with his handheld chain-saw running, whereupon the being retreated and floated up towards the craft in which other entities could now be seen. The worker grabbed at the creature's foot, only to have his hand burned. The alien entered the craft, which then promptly took off and vanished.

A year earlier, on 7 January 1970, two Finns who were resting during a cross-country ski run in a forest glade near Imjärvi, Heinola, had seen a domed disc appear overhead. From it, a beam of light was emitted vertically to the ground. Sparks danced where the beam hit the snow, and a small being suddenly appeared in the beam.

The creature had thin arms and legs, a hooked nose, green overalls and boots, a shining conical helmet, and was less than 3 feet (1 metre) tall. It aimed a 'box' at one of the men, Aarne Heinonen, and then both the beam and the entity faded upwards into the 'saucer' that, suddenly, was gone. Heinonen was ill for months after the incident.

Is Seeing Believing?

In the early hours of 12 October 1963, truck driver Eugenio Douglas was dazzled by a bright light on the road ahead of him near Monte Maíz, Córdoba, in Argentina. The truck ran into a ditch and Douglas climbed out to see a huge metallic object astride the road. Three robot-like beings, each of an estimated height of about 13 feet (4 metres), emerged from a door. They had helmets and suits that 'stuck to their bodies'. Douglas fired several shots at them, then fled. He was 'buzzed' by the UFO, which subjected him to prickling rays as he ran.

That same month, a woman living on Whidby Island, Washington, USA, also saw three occupants in a cylindrical UFO. One emerged through the side of the craft and approached her. It wore grey overalls with an aperture for eyes, but no eyes as such were visible. The being later returned to the craft in the same disconcerting manner.

One month later, on 16 November 1963, two young men from Kent, England, were walking with their girlfriends near Sandling Park in Saltwood, when they saw a bright 'star' descend, hover, and move among trees 80 yards (73 metres) away from them. The golden, oval-shaped UFO stopped and, instantly, a human-sized figure emerged and came shambling towards them. What they saw was completely black, and appeared to be headless, with wings like a bat. Panic seized the group of young people, and they fled.

In many of these cases, the UFOs and their occupants use beams of light and rays, or some kind of invisible force. Moreover, the instant appearances and instant retreats, and ghostlike walking through walls, seem to indicate that, in many cases, the witnesses were seeing images projected from intelligences within the craft. Later evidence also supports the idea that UFO occupants may have been selecting those with clairvoyant abilities and potential deep-trance subjects as their contacts.

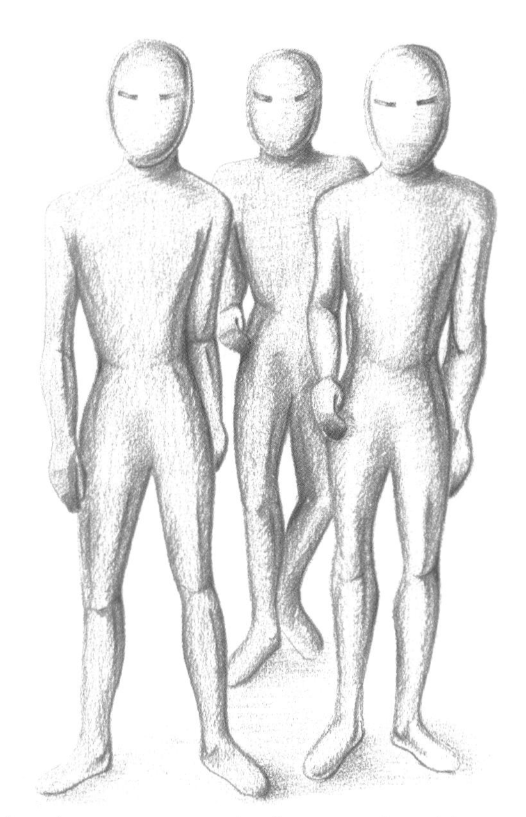

Witness Eugenio Douglas shot at the robot-like creatures,* right, *but they then fled into a UFO and disappeared.

The entity,* below, *confronted Aarne Heinonen in 1970 and made the reluctant witness ill for months.

In a brilliant series of articles entitled 'A long cool look at alien intelligence', which appeared in *Flying Saucer Review*, the author, C. Maxwell Cade, a radiation medicine specialist, suggested that UFO occupants could monitor witnesses' fears – perhaps of a hairy monster, for example. Such fears, amplified, could perhaps then be relayed back to the mind of the witness and – lo and behold! – a hairy monster actually appears!

Cade also points out that there are many ways of inducing hallucinations, from simple overdoses of alcohol, hypnotic suggestion and drugs (such as LSD) to irradiating the brain with high-frequency waves. If such techniques are within our grasp, then who can tell what mind-bending methods could be employed by superior intelligences?

> "The UFO mystery... expresses our secret longings for a wisdom that might come down from the stars in new, improved easy-to-use packaging..."
>
> **Jacques Vallee, Revelations: Alien Contact and Human Deception**

CRAZY NIGHT IN MAINE

EYES THAT TURNED ORANGE, A DETAILED MEDICAL EXAMINATION BY ALIENS AND SUBSEQUENT THREATS MARKED AN AMAZING EVENING'S JAUNT FOR TWO YOUNG AMERICANS

While Dr Herbert Hopkins, an American medical practitioner living in the state of Maine, was investigating a UFO case, he was allegedly visited by a weird 'man in black'. Subsequently, his son and daughter-in-law were also visited by a bizarre couple.

The case under investigation by Dr Hopkins at the time was a most extraordinary occurrence, involving two young Americans.

"THE CREATURE HAD HANDS AND FEET, WITH THREE WEBBED FINGERS AND A THUMB ON EACH HAND. THE HEAD WAS MUSHROOM-SHAPED, ITS LARGE, WHITE EYES WERE SLANTED ... AND NO MOUTH WAS VISIBLE. IT WORE A FLOWING BLACK SHEET-LIKE GARMENT."

While these young men watched what seemed to be hovering UFOs for several hours one night, they both experienced strange distortions of reality. Through the use of hypnosis, Hopkins subsequently elicited from one of the witnesses memories of having been being taken aboard an alien spacecraft and subjected to a medical examination of the kind that is common to so many reports of UFO contacts and close encounters.

The paranormal phenomena in the case were similar to those reported in many other sightings. The witnesses experienced obscure promptings that seemed to guide them to the encounter; and they thought that nearby farm animals – cows, ducks and geese – were also involved in the strange events. The psychic aspects of the case had been pursued by another investigator, Dr Berthold Schwarz, but without success.

The witnesses were terrified after their experience – to the point that they mistook stars and planets in the night sky for other UFOs. The two men were sincere, and investigating ufologists could find

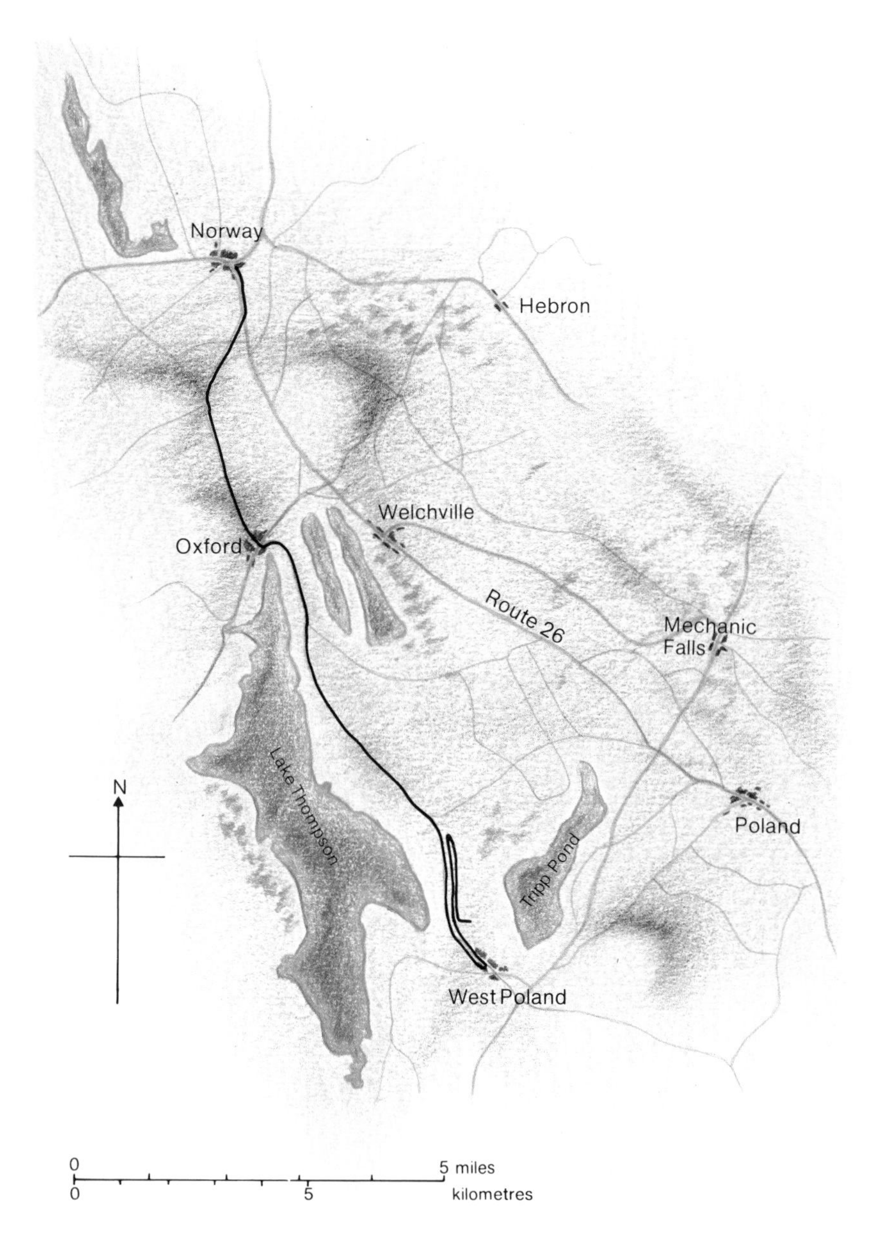

no explanation for the events of this crazy night, recounted here.

In October 1975, David Stephens, aged 21, and a friend aged 18 were sharing a trailer home in Norway, Maine, in the eastern United States. The two young men originally requested anonymity, but Stephens' name was subsequently revealed by an American UFO magazine. His friend's name was not revealed, however, so he will be referred to here as 'Paul'. They had known each other only a few weeks and had been struck by the fact that similar paranormal experiences had occurred to both of them.

Both David and Paul were working late shifts – David at a poultry processing plant, Paul at a wool mill – which is why they were both awake in the early hours of 27 October. They were listening to music at about 3 a.m. when they heard what sounded like an explosion. They rushed outside, but saw nothing unusual. While they were standing there,

On the map, above, 'X' marks the point where David Stephens and Paul watched UFO aerobatics over Tripp Pond during the night of their UFO encounter. The artist's impression,* left, *shows the strange spheres and cubes which they both sighted.

David suggested it would be a good night for a drive. Paul recommended a run down to nearby Lake Thompson. So they began driving southwards down Route 26. Their intention was to stay on that road until they were about 2 miles (3 kilometres) east of the town of Oxford. Then they would cut across to Oxford and go south alongside the lake.

RAPID JOURNEY

However, things did not work out like that. According to their subsequent statements, the car made a right turn on to a back road, against their will and with Paul gripping the steering wheel firmly. The road was a more direct route to Oxford, and was about 5 miles (8 kilometres) long. The ride was unusually smooth and they covered the distance very quickly, taking only about two minutes in all – implying that they were travelling at a speed that must have been in the region of 150 miles per hour (240 km/h).

After passing through Oxford, they continued down the eastern side of Lake Thompson where they noticed that cows in a field that they passed were shaking their heads from side to side. Just after that, they saw two beams of white light shining from a cornfield on to the road. Expecting to see a truck emerging, Paul slowed down. They were surprised to see the source of light rising from the ground. Coming to a halt, Paul switched off the car engine and they wound down the windows, expecting to see a helicopter. There was no sound. They saw instead a cylindrical shape rising behind the trees that fringed the field. It was surrounded by multicoloured lights that went out as the object lifted above the trees.

Alarmed, the two men restarted the car and accelerated away, closing the windows and locking the doors. Driving southwards, they then became aware of a beam of extremely bright light but had no conscious recollection of what happened next, until they found themselves in the car, parked on a track leading off from the tarred road on which they had been travelling, and close to the cornfield of the original sighting. The car windows were now partly opened, the doors were unlocked and they made an alarming discovery: David saw that Paul's eyes were 'all just orange', while Paul saw that David's were orange, except for the dark area of the pupils.

ENCOUNTER ON IMPULSE

The UFO still visible in the sky, David and Paul decided to drive on towards the town of West Poland. There they turned round and headed back along the same road. When they had gone about 2 miles (3 kilometres), the UFO was no longer visible. They turned back yet again, so that they were now travelling south. On an unexplained impulse, Paul again turned off the intended route, on to a gravel road leading down to Tripp Pond. As they completed the turn-off, they then saw the cylindrical object at an elevation of about 30 degrees from the horizontal and at an estimated distance of 150 to 200 yards (135 to 180 metres).

Suddenly, the car engine died and could not be restarted. The radio fell silent. Then the object moved 'in an up-and-down fashion' and took up a position at about 80 degrees of elevation in the south-east, at an estimated distance of 500 yards (450 metres).

David and Paul had been sitting in the immobile car for some 45 minutes when two disc-shaped objects appeared. They carried red, green and blue lights, and each was about a quarter of the size of the cylindrical craft. The discs then put on an 'aerobatic display', descending with a rocking motion, skimming the surface of Tripp Pond and rising swiftly, 'as though climbing a staircase'.

While all this was going on, the witnesses had the feeling that the pond, which in reality was half-a-mile (800 metres) distant, was only 20-30 feet (6-9 metres) away and immense, like an ocean. It seemed to them that there was an island over which the 'aerobatics' were taking place: but in fact, Tripp Pond has no such island.

Now fog began to form above the water. It approached and enveloped the car, but the cylinder was still visible. Meanwhile the radio burst into life – with a weather forecast, announcing that a bright and sunny day was in store.

At 6.30 a.m., Paul tried again to start the car. This time he was successful, and by 7 a.m., they arrived at the home of David's family in Oxford. The dreamlike quality of the experience and the ominous significance that seemed to invest every small incident are brought out in remarks made by David:

'What was weird was when the big one went straight up, the clouds seemed to follow it. It just took off, and all this time not a car went by. We didn't see a person, or an animal, or a bird ... nothing! And when the cloud disappeared, two ducks went by and then two geese went by and then two ducks again went by. They were going in twos, and we noticed the cows were getting up in twos'.

Surprisingly, the pair made a return journey to Tripp Pond at 4 p.m. on 28 October, when what seemed like snowflakes began to fall around them and strange cubes and spheres apparently 'whizzed in all directions'.

Threats from a Stranger

The following morning, David Stephens was alone in the trailer when he was disturbed by a loud knocking on the door. When he opened it, he found himself face to face with a stockily built man who sported a crew-cut hairstyle, sunglasses and dark blue clothing. He asked David if he was the one who had seen a 'flying saucer'. When David confirmed this, the stranger said: 'Better keep your mouth shut if you know what's good for you'. He then scurried away around an adjacent building, and no more was seen of him.

The Stephens family reported the UFO encounter to the Androscoggin County Sheriff and then to the *Lewiston Daily Sun*. After making initial enquiries, a UFO investigator, Shirley Fickett, taped interviews with the witnesses on 11 November. She was interested in the time that was 'lost' after the intense beam of light had struck the car and rendered its occupants unconscious. She wanted to have the witnesses questioned under hypnosis and learned that Dr Herbert Hopkins sometimes used hypnosis in the treatment of his patients. In a spirit of scientific adventure, Dr Hopkins offered his services free of charge.

The artist's impression,* above, *shows one of the strange creatures who took blood from David Stephens and subjected him to a thorough medical.

Dr Berthold Schwarz,* below, *studied the contact witness David Stephens, finding him to have much in common with other contactees and with gifted psychics – energy, individualism and pent-up tension.

David Stephens was the first to be questioned. His parents, Mrs Fickett and Paul were present. But Paul later refused to attend any further sessions and withdrew completely from the investigations. Eight hypnotic sessions were conducted from December to March 1976. Under hypnosis, David described standing outside the car after the light beam had struck it: he felt that he was standing on a 'floor suspended above', watching through a window as the car slid sideways, with Paul still in it. He was in a room with curved walls. At first he was alone, but he was joined after a while by what appeared to be a non-human being. The creature had hands and feet, with three webbed fingers and a thumb on each hand. The head was mushroom-shaped, its large, white eyes were slanted, its nose was small, and no mouth was visible. The creature wore a flowing black sheet-like garment. It communicated not by voice but by 'brain waves' with David, whose name it somehow knew.

Blood Samples

David was then taken into another room where there were four similar beings. It was like a 'hospital room with an operating table'. Blood – enough to fill two syringes – was taken from near his right elbow. When the beings tried to persuade him to lie on the table for a medical examination, David became violent and struck one of them. They did not retaliate, and eventually he relented. He was divested of his clothes and thoroughly examined, from head to toe, with a box-like device. The creatures seemed to want to be friendly. When David was at last returned to the car, Paul seemed unaware that he had ever been away.

In the final hypnotic session, David seemed to suffer great emotional conflict when he was questioned about a statement made by the beings, to the effect that they would return. He could not, or would not, disclose anything on this point, and the questioning was discontinued because of his obvious distress.

When Dr Berthold Schwarz conducted his psychiatric-parapsychological investigation, he concluded that there had been no previous interest on David Stephens' part in flying saucers, or detailed knowledge of any classic cases, in spite of an interest in the paranormal. He also concluded that David was still frightened and puzzled by the events, that there were no contradictions in his story, and that there was no history or evidence of dishonesty or loss of memory before these events.

Concerning the medical examination, Dr Schwarz stated that it seemed so absurd technically that 'one wonders if this wasn't staged by the UFO forces in order to create a particular impression'. He noted, in connection with the orange colour of witnesses' eyes at one point, that an ophthalmologist had said that, when he used a substance known as *fluorescein* in the course of his work, the eyes became transiently orange.

Using their 'brain wave' system of communication, the entities had told David Stephens that they would return. Did they perhaps do so, in the guise of the weird 1930s-style character who attempted to scare off Dr Herbert Hopkins – an investigator who had perhaps learned too much?

ALIEN SPACECRAFT – HALLUCINATIONS OR FRAUD? HERE, WE LOOK AT VARIOUS POSSIBLE EXPLANATIONS, AND CONSIDER WHETHER THE PHENOMENON POSSIBLY LIES OUTSIDE OUR USUAL CATEGORIES OF THOUGHT

UFOs – ASSESSING THE EVIDENCE

Alien beings must exist somewhere in the Universe, in some form or other. Of this, there is little doubt. The problem confronting us is therefore whether the evidence we possess proves that some of them are visiting the Earth right now. If this is so, then proving the fact would be of the utmost significance, and would certainly constitute the most momentous occasion in the history of the world.

Unfortunately, we do not possess reliable photographs, movie films or tape recordings of aliens, or artefacts manufactured in another world... or anything that goes beyond mere testimony. In view of this paucity of hard evidence, we can hardly say, with any definiteness, whether aliens are or are not visiting us. Instead, we can only make a reasoned assessment of the facts.

The dilemmas posed by close encounters of the fourth kind are starkly illustrated by a case that occurred in the north of England on 28 November 1980. Police Constable Alan Godfrey had been called out to pursue some cows that were allegedly roaming a housing estate. By 5.15 a.m., still not having found them, he was ready to give up the search. Then, while making one last trip in his patrol car before coming off duty, he saw a glow on the road ahead. He instantly thought of a works bus that regularly travelled the route and idly wondered why it was a little early. Then, as he approached the glow, it became obvious that he had been wrong.

The object that confronted PC Godfrey was like a spinning top with windows. It was hovering just above the road surface, spanning the gap between two lamp posts, and was rotating. He could see his headlights reflected in its metallic surface, and that leaves on the roadside bushes were moving in the vortex created by its rotation. The road surface, soaking wet in other places, was dry in blotchy patches directly beneath the object. There was no doubt in his mind that the object was real.

Keeping calm, the officer propped his clipboard on the windscreen and carefully sketched the object. But then something inexplicable happened. He suddenly found himself further down the road, driving the car away from the scene. He turned the car round and drove back past the spot, now deserted, where the object had been. He then carried on the short distance into town and collected a colleague. Only at this point did he notice the time. Somehow, since the moment he first saw the UFO, all of 10 minutes had disappeared.

This was not all. Constable Godfrey reported having a dim memory of a strange voice saying: 'This is not for your eyes. You will forget it.' Additional fragmentary recollections gradually filtered back to him until, nine months after the incident, and with the help of ufologists, he underwent regression hypnosis. This was conducted by an eminently qualified and rather sceptical psychiatrist, but what appeared to be a coherent memory of the incident emerged.

The story was of the usual type: the officer had been taken on board the UFO and given a medical examination by two distinct types of humanoid creature – one tall, the other small and somewhat ugly. Remarkably, this is almost exactly what the Day family claimed happened to them during their abduction at Aveley in Essex. In fact, contact cases reported from Britain share many such similar features. Cases reported from other countries show similarities among themselves, too.

What happened to the police constable? Did he lie? If not, did he have an hallucination or did he undergo the events he described? Or was it something between an hallucination and a straightforward experience – a distortion or misinterpretation of some extraordinary event?

In the north of England, a craft resembling a spinning top, **left,** *hovers above a road. The witness was a police constable, Alan Godfrey, seen* **below left.** *Later, he recalled the experience of being taken aboard the craft, where he was examined by terrifying creatures.*

There happens to be unusual and powerful support for the 'face-value' interpretation of the story. Four police officers on patrol 8 miles (13 kilometres) away had to duck as an object streaked low over their heads, moving directly towards the town near which the encounter took place. And a caretaker lighting a school's boilers saw, in the direction of the town, an object that fitted PC Godfrey's description, climbing into the sky. These stories were reported.

There are many questions posed by reports of alien sightings. Why should aliens look like us? Why do they behave like us? Why do they never tell us anything valuable to which we do not already have access? Taken together, these facts seem to suggest a mental origin for these strange experiences.

Research into lucid dreams has also proved revealing as far as supposed sightings are concerned. These are dreams in which the dreamer knows he is dreaming. Often, the course of the dream can be controlled by conscious effort.

Although they seem so real at the time, lucid dreams give away their 'unreal' nature by means of various subtle hints. For example, the subject does not react with normal responses. He may feel no fear, despite the weirdness of the experience. He will not wake up a sleeping partner to witness the events. In one case, a lucid dream was of an atomic bomb exploding in a garden. The subject's response was to yawn and fall asleep. The behaviour of contact case witnesses is often just like this.

Sensory Deprivation

Interestingly, such symptoms also occur in hallucinations that follow long periods of sensory deprivation. When a person is kept in darkness and silence, and even his sense of touch is deprived of normal stimulation because his hands are enveloped in special gloves, the mind starts to manufacture its own 'perceptions' – hallucinations of sound, sight and touch. When we consider the usual setting of certain contacts – night-time, a tired driver, a lonely country road, and the sudden appearance of a slightly unusual sight, such as a bright light in the sky – it does not stretch credulity very far to suggest that these could be hallucinations brought about by lack of sensory stimulation.

In the USA, Dr Alvin Lawson, a professor of English at the University of California, conducted experiments that are relevant to the hallucination theory. He advertised for people of a 'creative' turn of mind to take part in an unspecified experiment. He screened out all those who seemed to have a knowledge of, or interest in, UFOs. The rest were asked to imagine, under hypnosis, that they were being abducted by aliens. They were led on with certain key questions, and the results, he claimed, were so closely akin to the stories told of allegedly

InFocus

WORDS OF WISDOM?

In 1976, an American contactee group published a letter which they said had been channelled by telepathy from outer space. Addressed to Terrestrial Brother Carter (U.S. President at the time), it warned him: 'Remember, do not do as others have done! We remind you that this authority has been granted from above... your action could render it constructive and effective, prosperous, salvaging light for all mankind. Remember, Jimmy Carter, Remember! From the Heavens to Earth.'

Such a message is something of an exception. Surveying 16 years of editing *Flying Saucer Review,* Charles Bowen commented on the general absurdities featured in alien messages. In 1968, in Argentina, two 'men' with transparent legs gave a farmer's son a message, rendered as: 'You shall know the world. F. Saucer.'

In 1965, in Venezuela, two beings, said to be 7 to 8 feet (2.1 – 2.4 metres) tall, with long, yellow hair and protruding eyes, were asked whether there were 'any human beings like you living among us?' The answer was: 'Yes. 2,417,805.'

During the 1954 'flap', a French witness encountered a small being standing before a glowing disc-shaped craft. The alien repeated several times in a mechanical voice: 'La veritée est refusée aux constipés,' and 'Ce que vous appelez cancer vient des dents.' Translated, these messages from another civilisation read: 'Truth is denied to the constipated' (or 'to the ill at ease'), and 'That which is known as cancer comes from the teeth' (or 'through what you eat').

THE TROUBLE WITH HYPNOSIS

In 1977, Professor Alvin Lawson began to investigate the validity of UFO abduction reports obtained under hypnosis. He hypnotised a total of 16 volunteers who knew very little about UFOs. Once in trance, they were asked to imagine a series of events – seeing a UFO, being taken on board, given an examination, and so on. Lawson hoped to find differences between their imaginary accounts and those given by alleged UFO contactees. Such differences would enhance the credibility of the 'real' reports.

To his surprise, it was the similarities that were most striking. For example, among his test subjects' narratives were descriptions of tubes of light, which extended from UFOs or retracted into them, perhaps levitating the subject aboard.

Sometimes, the subject described the UFO imagined during the hypnotic trance as 'getting bigger and smaller'. Patterns of pulsating colours, rotating spirals and geometric patterns were also often reported. All these features are common in 'real' UFO reports, but they are rare in science fiction stories and films, a likely source of UFO imagery.

The experiments showed that authentic-sounding reports could be produced in abundance during trance states by subjects asked to imagine close encounters, but who have never claimed to have been abducted by a UFO. Dr Lawson concluded that contact case witnesses were not lying – but he could offer no hypothesis as to the nature of the stimulus causing their experiences.

P E R S P E C T I V E S

'real' abductions that it was likely that these also were, wholly or in part, subconscious fantasies.

Such different types of evidence constitute impressive support for the contention that alien contacts are hallucinatory. But there is a fair amount of negative evidence too. Some contact experiences are shared. But while collective hallucinations can occur, they are not well-understood, and some encounters stretch this hypothesis to breaking-point. One Italian case involved as many as seven witnesses; one British case involved four. In some cases, meanwhile, such as those in Puerto Rico and that involving the English police officer, there is at least some degree of independent corroboration.

Alvin Lawson's work, as he himself recognised, showed major differences between allegedly 'real' abductions and imagined ones, as well as similarities. When, in a UFO contact case, memories emerge by way of hypnosis, they are almost invariably associated with very strong emotions, more consistent with the memory of a real event than a fantasy. The 'abductions' imagined in the laboratory did not display this effect; and in general those who took part in the experiment knew afterwards that

> " THE GREATER THE EDUCATION, THE HIGHER THE PROPORTION THAT INDICATED THEY HAVE HEARD OF FLYING SAUCERS, WHO THINK THEY ARE REAL RATHER THAN THE PRODUCT OF IMAGINATION AND WHO BELIEVE THAT THERE ARE PEOPLE SOMEWHAT LIKE OURSELVES LIVING ON OTHER PLANETS... "
>
> **ALDORA LEE, COLORADO UNIVERSITY REPORT**

Alpha Centauri, **right**, *a well-dressed science fiction monster from the television series* Dr Who, *is more outlandish than most descriptions of aliens provided by UFO contactees. 'Real' ufonauts are far more similar to human beings – or to gnomes, giants, dwarves and other traditional mythical creatures.*

Two high officials of the Draconian race, **left**, *are another instance of the television designer's imagination outstripping the diversity of reported aliens. Animal forms, or hybrid animal-human forms like these, might be expected among ufonauts – whether they were genuinely extra-terrestrial or the products of the human imagination. In fact, both 'real' accounts and 'imaginary' ones, produced under laboratory conditions, are seldom of this type.*

they had been fantasising. Contact witnesses, however, are never in any doubt that their regression memory is of a 'real' event.

We must also consider the frequent reports of physical effects on the body of a witness, such as burns on the skin. Marks on the ground sometimes accompany these cases. But, on the other hand, there is almost no photographic support for contact witnesses' stories, and it is known that physical effects can be produced psychosomatically.

Looking at more subtle features of such accounts, considerable consistency and a kind of lucid cohesiveness appear in all but certain 'bedroom visitor' cases. This tends to make the UFO investigator doubt that he is dealing with experiences more akin to dreams than reality.

Perhaps the fairest judgement we can make at present is to say that some such experiences seem more like vivid hallucinations than reality. Some cases have elements suggesting hallucinations but may offer data that casts doubt on this assumption. Some also seem to be of a unique type, almost a hybrid between dreams and reality.

So what of the other extreme? Are these contacts extra-terrestrial in nature? This, the 'face-value' hypothesis, implies that hundreds of different races (most of them not very imaginative variants on ourselves), from many different worlds, are taking a great deal of interest in the Earth. They perform medical examinations interminably, and gather up endless cargoes of soil and rock samples.

Sceptics invariably ask why the aliens fail to contact anyone important. Why do they not land on the White House lawn and thus dispel all doubts? Contactee Gaynor Sunderland asked Arna, one of the aliens she claimed to have met, this very question. In reply, she was told that people in authority had so much credibility to lose that there was no point in contacting them, although this had been tried on a few occasions. Fear of the consequences always kept such people silent. Instead, the aliens prefer to pursue a policy of contacting children or simple folk, knowing that some of these will brave ridicule and speak out.

This argument makes an intriguing amount of sense. A slow, covert process of conditioning world opinion to the idea of extra-terrestrial visitors fits well with the provocative, but not probative, evidence that we possess. Solid proof would be detrimental to such a policy: it might be impounded, or hidden, or denied outright. Suggestive indications, on the other hand, avoid the unwelcome attention of authority, while providing a stimulus to continued interest and the long, slow build-up of belief. Even the confusing and ridiculous behaviour of aliens would fit this theory.

A great deal of fascinating work remains to be done before we can even hope to know the truth. There is no hard evidence that a superior intelligence has made contact with the Earth – but we do have suggestive hints that this might be true. And, since most of us would probably wish UFOs to come from space, our judgement is clouded by an enormous emotional bias.

> "IF SUCH THINGS AS UFOs... DID NOT EXIST AS A POSSIBILITY, THEN THE WORLD WOULD BE A DULL PLACE TO LIVE IN... DOES IT REALLY MATTER THAT 90 PER CENT ARE NOT TRUE UFOs?"
>
> **JENNY RANDLES AND PETER WARRINGTON, UFOS: A BRITISH VIEWPOINT**

***Of the six drawings* below, *three were made by witnesses in UFO contact cases, and were offered as bona fide representations of alien beings. The others were made by participants in Alvin Lawson's 'simulated abduction' experiments. These subjects, though they produced their accounts under hypnosis, were never in doubt about the imaginary nature of their experiences. Is there a different 'feel' about the two types of drawing? Can you pick out the three 'real' contact witness drawings? The answer is printed at the* lower right.**

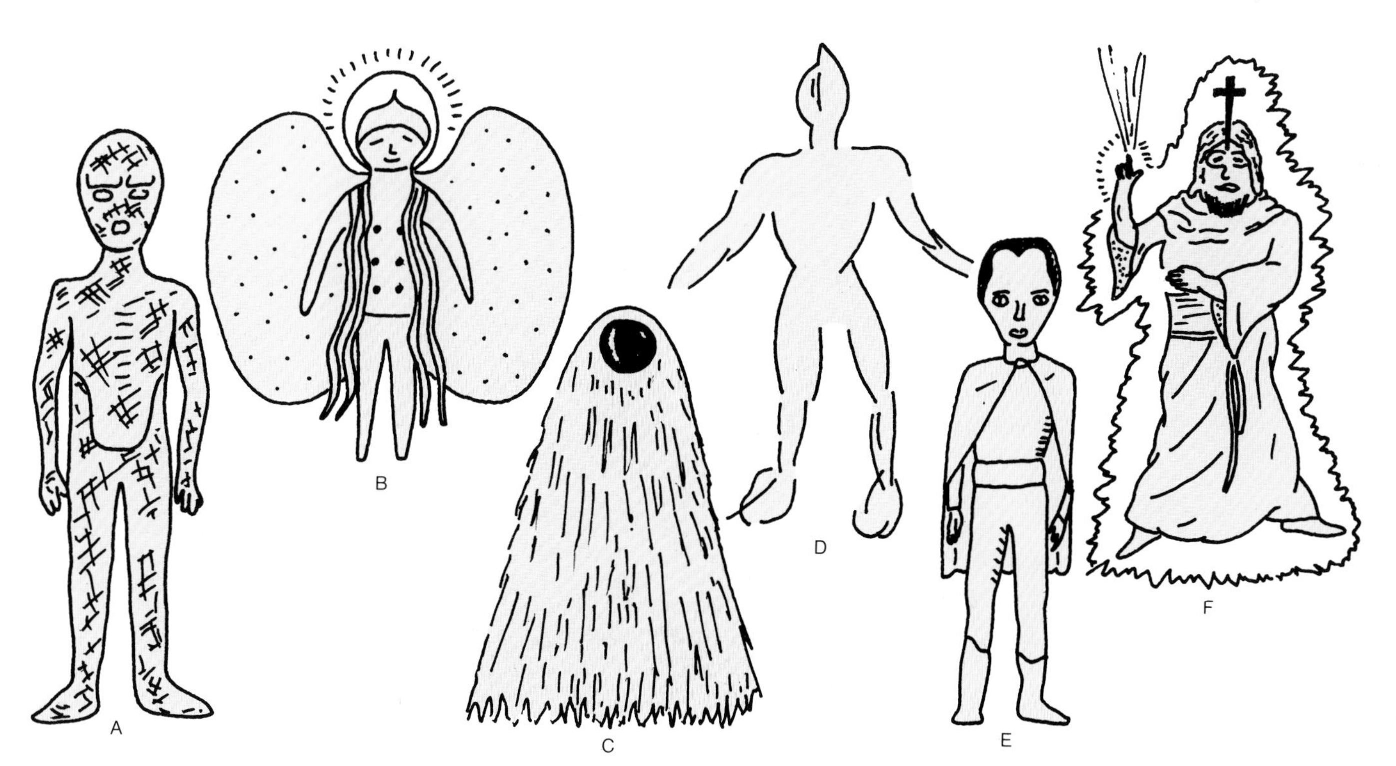

Answer: B, E, F

CRASHED TO EARTH?

EVER SINCE THE TERM 'FLYING SAUCER' WAS COINED IN 1947, THERE HAVE BEEN RUMOURS THAT THE US GOVERNMENT HAS ONE OR MORE CRASHED UFOS – COMPLETE WITH ALIEN PILOTS – IN ITS CUSTODY. WHAT EVIDENCE IS THERE FOR THIS INTRIGUING IDEA?

Towards the end of 1988, a group of Soviet military men, flying in a helicopter near Dal'negorsk in the far east of the USSR, noticed a strange object on the ground. After landing to investigate, they found a cylindrical object about 19 feet (six metres) long, which did not look like any part of a conventional aircraft. Unable to lift it, they decided to return the following spring, but by then the object had vanished.

Reports of crashed UFOs have made news ever since the first reports of 'flying saucers' in 1947. At that time a rumour circulated that a UFO had crashed and was under examination by American scientists. It was logical enough: given the great number reported to be around, it seemed statistically certain that sooner or later one of them would suffer an accident, or be shot down.

Such reasoning assumed that the UFOs were solid, material objects, liable to physical accident or mechanical malfunction. In those early days, there was little question in anyone's mind that the UFOs were as solid as terrestrial aircraft: the only question was as to where they originated.

What threw the crashed saucer legend into disrepute was, paradoxically, a book that set out to establish it as fact. In 1950, an American writer named Frank Scully brought out *Behind the Flying Saucers,* a bestseller in both the USA and Europe. Something of the contemporary climate of opinion comes over in the dust-cover blurb: 'It is typical of the whole extraordinary and delightful business of the flying saucers that the first person to attempt a serious book about them should be the show business magazine *Variety's* ace columnist.' (The point could have been made even more strongly by mentioning that Scully was also the author of *Fun in Bed* – not a sex manual, but a collection of diversions for the bedridden – which was sufficiently successful to be followed by *More Fun in Bed* and *Junior Fun in Bed.*) True, there were few serious ufologists around in 1950; but Scully's credentials did nothing to enhance the credibility of his story.

The story Scully had to tell needed all the support it could get. In the course of his professional writing, he claimed, he had come across a Texas oilman named Silas Newton who, in turn, told Scully of his colleague 'Dr Gee' – who, he alleged, had first-hand knowledge of three UFOs that were held in the custody of the United States military, along with 16 dead occupants, about 3 feet (1 metre) tall. No supportive evidence was produced: it all

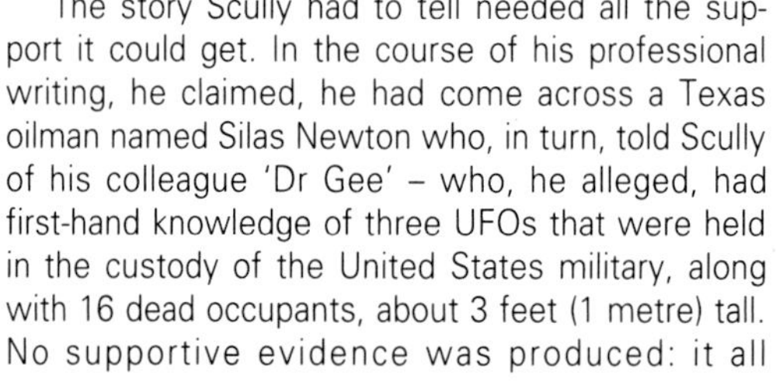

PERSPECTIVES

ALIENS, DEAD AND ALIVE

Most descriptions of aliens recovered from crashed UFOs conjure up creatures that are very human-like. A crash in the New Mexico desert, west of Socorro, in July 1947, has given rise to several extraordinary reports about the craft's occupants. A civil engineer who encountered the 'disc-shaped aircraft' described the dead aliens as having round heads that were larger in proportion to their bodies than in humans, small eyes that were oddly spaced, and no hair. 'Their clothing,' he said, 'seemed to be one-piece and grey in colour. You couldn't see any zippers, belts or buttons...'

The New Mexico aliens were also claimed to have been seen by a Sergeant Melvin E. Brown while at Roswell Army Air Field in the same year, 1947. Some of the materials collected from the site of the crash were put in refrigerated trucks and Sergeant Brown and another were ordered to guard one of the vehicles. Overcome by curiosity, they looked under the tarpaulin to see what had been packed in the ice and saw three bodies.

They were, said Sergeant Brown, 'friendly looking and had nice faces.' Apparently, they looked Asian – possibly even Chinese because of their slanted eyes – but had larger heads and were hairless.

The most amazing report, however, comes from a man who was in the area of the crash at the time; then, he was but a five-year-old searching for moss agate stones together with members of his family. He claims to have come across three aliens lying underneath a silver disc on the side of a hill.

Measuring about four feet long, with unusually large heads and 'almond-shaped, coal black eyes', they lay quite still. One had trouble breathing, while a fourth alien sitting nearby 'recoiled in fear, like it thought we were going to attack it.' The man and his family were eventually hustled away by US soldiers.

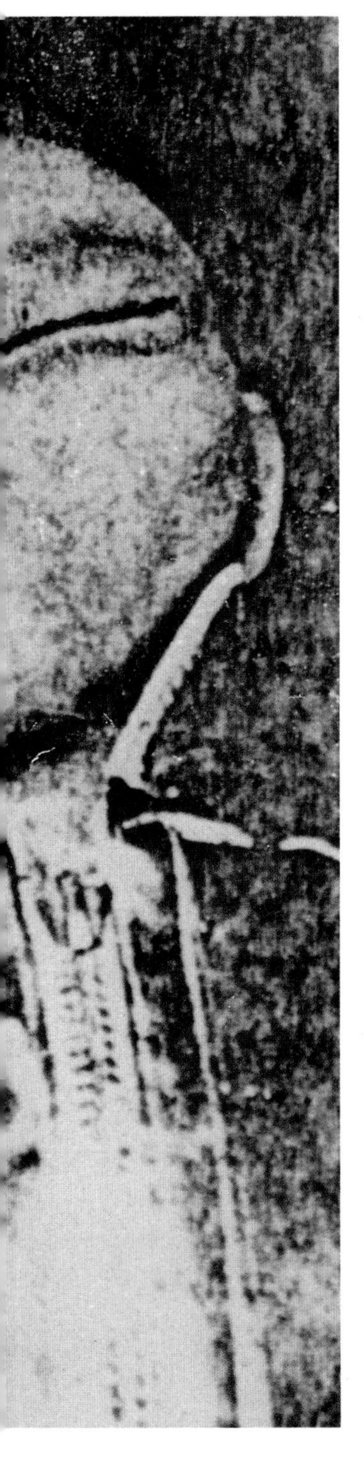

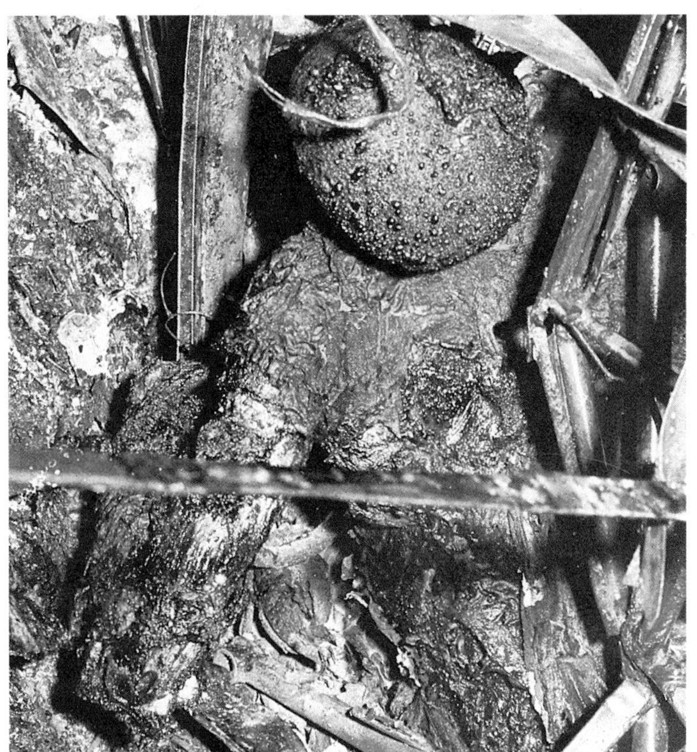

The photograph, **left**, *is of an alleged dead alien, retrieved from a UFO that crashed in New Mexico on 7 July 1948.*

A flying saucer collides with the Washington Monument in a still, **below**, *from the 1956 movie* **Earth vs Flying Saucers**. *However advanced the technology of UFOs, there is surely no reason why they should not sometimes crash. And if they do, then surely it is natural for the military to take an interest?*

depended on the word of 'Dr Gee', who claimed to have been one of the scientists called in by the authorities to examine the UFOs.

This drawback did not prevent Scully's book selling more than 60,000 copies; but it did mean that when, two years later, journalist J.P. Kahn wrote an article pointing out the weaknesses of Scully's story, he found it easy enough to persuade the world that it was a total fabrication. The fact that Kahn's exposé was itself full of exaggerations and inaccuracies was overlooked: it made its point, namely that Scully had taken the story on trust and done virtually no independent research. Newton and 'Dr Gee' were labelled frauds.

It was not until some 25 years later that the crashed saucer legend surfaced again. In April 1976, there appeared in the pages of *Official UFO* (at that time, a fairly serious journal) an article entitled 'What about crashed UFOs?', by the widely respected investigator Raymond Fowler. Instead of serving up again the vague rumours of the past, he produced dramatic new evidence in the form of a technician's sworn statement that he had personally examined a crashed UFO at Kingman, Arizona, on 21 May 1953.

A model of what is believed to be an alien corpse that was recovered in New Mexico in July 1947 and placed in a zippered body-bag, is shown **above**.

The Roswell Incident

From then on, interest in the subject became very serious and intense. Another investigator of repute, Leonard Stringfield, dedicated himself to the search for further evidence; and while he ranged far and wide in his quest, two other men, William Moore and Stanton Friedman, in conjunction with Charles Berlitz, concentrated on a single case that was soon to become famous – the Roswell incident.

The story, in outline, is as follows. Sitting outside their home on the night of 2 July 1947, a couple at Roswell, New Mexico, saw a glowing object streak across the sky. The next morning, about 75 miles (120 kilometres) further on in the direction of its path, a rancher found extraordinary debris scattered over his ground. A further 150 miles (240 kilometres) or so away, an engineer and some archaeologists came across the remains of an unidentifiable flying object, together with several strange bodies. The authorities took control, announced that the object was simply a weather balloon, and nothing more was heard of the matter – until Moore, Friedman and Berlitz took up the case, that is.

Other incidents, uncannily similar in some respects, abound. On 7 July 1948, near Del Rio, Texas, USA, for instance, unusual radar sightings led to the suspicion that an unidentified flying

In 1953, a metallurgist named Daly, who worked at the Wright-Patterson Air Force Base in Ohio, was sent on a secret mission to examine what appeared to be a flying saucer. After carrying out tests on the craft – as shown in the artist's impression,* right *– he concluded it must be of extraterrestrial origin.

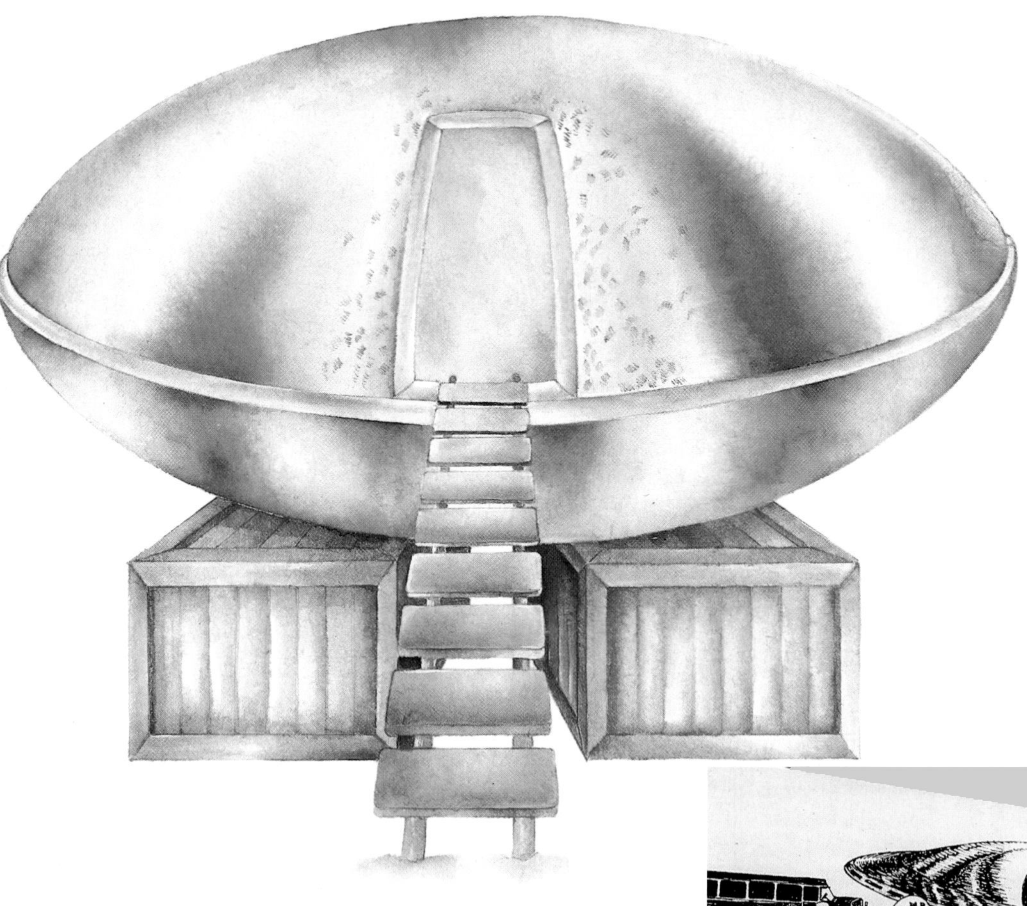

A crashed UFO in the Arizona desert is shown illuminated by the glare of spotlights in the sketch,* centre right. *A civilian engineer, known by the pseudonym Fritz Werner, brought in to calculate the object's speed of impact, noticed the body of a small humanoid figure in a metallic suit. In 1973, Werner signed an affidavit testifying that this incident had occurred to him 20 years before.

object had crashed some 30 miles (50 kilometres) across the Mexican border. With permission from the Mexican government, US troops went to investigate, and found a metallic disc, together with the burned bodies of the crew, more or less human-like beings about 5 feet (1.5 metres) tall. The object, which had been clocked at 2,000 miles per hour (3,200 km/h) by radar, had been seen simultaneously on radar by USAF Colonel Whitcomb in an F94 jet fighter. He landed at his home base and immediately took off for the scene in a borrowed light aircraft. Here, he found Mexican troops in control, and the object hidden from sight. But a naval intelligence officer arrived in time to see the crash area roped off and some objects being loaded on to trucks.

The troops taking part had apparently been warned that, if they spoke of the matter, they would be 'the sorriest people around'. Photographs, allegedly of the bodies of the occupants, were circulating clandestinely some years later, and continue to be the subject of controversial debate.

Official reaction was no less threatening when, in 1952, at the Muroc (now Edwards) Air Force Base in California, a USAF radar operator tracked an object descending towards Earth at great speed. After a crash had been confirmed, he was instructed: 'You didn't see anything'. Later he learned that a UFO, more than 17 yards (16 metres) in diameter, had crashed in a desert area not far away. It was metallic, and badly burned; and it contained bodies of beings about 5 feet (1.5 metres) tall. The debris was kept for a while at the base, then allegedly shipped to the Wright-Patterson Air Force Base at Dayton in Ohio. There is strong evidence that some object was indeed secretly shipped to the Wright-Patterson base.

Possibly relating to the same incident is a five-minute film that was shown the following spring, apparently by the military authorities, to a select group, including a radar specialist with security clearance, who was working at the time for the army and air force, stationed at Fort Monmouth, New Jersey. The movie showed a silver disc-shaped object embedded in the sand in a remote desert area. It had a dome on top, and an open hatch or door. Some 10-15 military personnel could be seen standing near the craft. Its diameter, based on a comparison of its size with that of the human figures, appeared to be 6-8 yards (5-7 metres). The film also showed the bodies of three

CASEBOOK

FRAGMENTARY EVIDENCE

In June 1952, six Norwegian army jets on summer manoeuvres over the inhospitable islands of Spitzbergen, *right,* in the Arctic Ocean, spotted wreckage in a mountain area near the Hinlopen Straits. Within hours, using ski-planes, Norwegian investigators – among them, an expert on rocketry – were on site. No doubt, a Soviet vehicle or missile was suspected, but instead they found the wreckage of a disc-shaped object, with 46 jet-like orifices on the rim. The object

dead occupants: they were small and human-like, with over-large heads. The group was told to think about the film but not to tell anyone about it. Two weeks later, they were told it was a hoax. This seems strange, for there is a certain amount of evidence that the film was shown to officers at a number of military bases. Clearly someone, somewhere, felt that it was important for them to see it. Quite apart from the poor quality of the film – which, paradoxically, tends to suggest it is genuine – the cost in time and effort of setting up such an elaborate fake must have been formidable.

> " IF UFOS HAVE CRASHED, AND ALIENS ... ARE IN CUSTODY, IT IS SURELY TIME THAT THE AUTHORITIES LET US INTO SUCH SECRETS. "

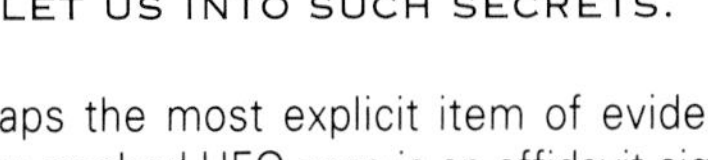

Perhaps the most explicit item of evidence in the entire crashed UFO saga is an affidavit signed in 1973 by a certain Fritz Werner – a pseudonym, although his true identity is known – who swore that he had assisted at the investigation into a crashed unknown object. While serving as project engineer on an air force contract near Kingman, Arizona, in 1953, he was given an assignment. Along with some 15 others, he was taken early one morning under strict security conditions in a blacked-out bus on a five-hour journey. He and his companions were then told that a super-secret air force craft had crashed, and that each of them was to investigate the crash in terms of his specific field of expertise.

Werner described the object as like two deep saucers, one inverted on the other, about 11 yards (10 metres) in diameter, made of dull silver metal, with an open hatch to the interior. His particular task was to calculate the object's impact velocity from the traces. He found no landing gear, and no dents or scratches. In a tent nearby, he saw a dead humanoid, about 4 feet 3 inches (1.3 metres) in height, on a table. Not only were the investigators instructed to tell nobody of the incident, they were not even allowed to discuss it among themselves.

Another incident from 1953 that seems to confirm the Fritz Werner report is the case of a metallurgist named Daly who worked for the air force at the Wright-Patterson AFB, Ohio. He described being taken to a location, unidentified but abounding in hot sand. (For the last part of his journey, he was blindfolded.) For two days, he was required to examine the structure of a silvery metallic craft lying undamaged in the sand. He concluded it was not of earthly origin; what is more, he saw no sign of occupants.

Despite obvious discrepancies, these two reports may relate to the same incident. Relevant, too, may be the evidence given by the wife of a guard at Wright-Patterson. She alleged that, at about this time, her husband had witnessed scientists examining the bodies of large-headed humanoids, about 3 feet (1 metre) in height.

Another incident, two years later, at the Wright-Patterson base, also appears to confirm that pilots of crashed spacecraft were taken there for examination. A woman, whose duty was to catalogue all incoming material relating to UFOs, stated that she had seen the bodies of two dead humanoids, about 5 feet (1.5 metres) tall, with large heads, being transferred from one location to another.

SOUTH AMERICAN MYSTERIES

In March 1964, it was reported that a round, flat UFO, giving off a bright blue and orange light, had crashed high on Mount Chitpec, Mexico. Officials wanted to take it to the nearest town, San Cristóbal de las Casas; but the local tribe, the Chalulas, insisted it was a gift from God and the Virgin, and refused to allow its removal.

Some years later, in May 1978, many people in Tarija, in the most remote and inaccessible part of Bolivia, saw a glowing object cross the afternoon sky. It was generally described as a metallic cylinder, some 8 or 9 yards (7 or 8 metres) in length, without windows or structural details, and closely followed by another, smaller object. A few seconds later, there was the sound of a great explosion, accompanied by an 'earthquake' that registered on seismic equipment over some 77,000 square miles (200,000 square kilometres). After the crash, the smaller object was seen to fly away.

The object's rate of travel was far too slow for it to have been a meteor, and investigation subsequently ruled out the possibility of a satellite returning to Earth. But while speculation bubbled in the press, a security blackout was officially imposed. Reporters saw the object removed by technicians, and asserted that it had been taken by the United States Air Force back to the USA. NASA denied any knowledge of this – as, of course, it would have done even if it had been involved.

The evidence presented in such incidents is often far from convincing; yet it is hard to discount it altogether. To assert that every one of these reports is a lie, or a misinterpretation of some simple event, is to call into question a great number of witnesses, unknown to one another and wholeheartedly trusted by experienced investigators. If UFOs have indeed crashed, and aliens – dead or alive – are in custody, it is surely time that the authorities let us into such secrets.

seemed to be made of an unknown metal, and there was no trace of occupants.

What is perhaps the most remarkable aspect of this incident is the comment made by a high-ranking army officer, Colonel Gernod Darnbyl of the Norwegian general staff, who later said: 'The crashing of the Spitzbergen disc was highly important. Although our present scientific knowledge does not permit us to solve all the riddles, I am confident that these remains from Spitzbergen will be of utmost importance. Some time ago, a misunderstanding was caused by saying that this disc probably was of Soviet origin. We wish to state categorically that it was not built by any country on Earth. The materials used in its construction are completely unknown to the experts who took part in the investigation'.

HERALDS OF THE ANTICHRIST?

UFOLOGISTS HAVE OFTEN NOTED CLOSE PARALLELS BETWEEN DEVILS WHICH, IN THE MEDIEVAL PERIOD, WERE BELIEVED TO BE REAL, AND THE OCCUPANTS OF MODERN UFOs. BUT DOES THIS REALLY MEAN THAT EXTRA-TERRESTRIALS ARE ESSENTIALLY EVIL?

***Demons are seen torturing their victims in hell, in a 16th-century illustration from a French manuscript,* below.**

On 18 March 1978, Bill Herrmann, a 30-year-old truck driver of Charleston, South Carolina, USA, was watching what he subsequently described as a 'slick metal disc, about sixty feet [18.3 metres] in diameter', as it manoeuvred in the sky near his home. Abruptly, it dropped towards him. 'Suddenly, it was right in front of me. I fell backwards. The next thing I knew, there was light all around me, green and blue, and I felt myself being tugged upward.'

In what seemed to him only a moment, Herrmann found himself sitting miles away in an open field, within a diminishing circle of orange light, as the spacecraft skittered away in a triangular flight pattern that, he was told later, had been designed to prevent damage from Earth radar sources. 'I couldn't remember anything. I didn't know where I was. A terrible fear came over me, and I stood there weeping for what seemed a long time. I felt dirty. I felt like . . . I can't describe it. I felt like I had been around something I shouldn't have been around.'

Later, under hypnosis, Herrmann recalled an examining table, flashing lights, and creatures resembling human foetuses, with over-large heads and eyes, spongy white skin, and wearing rust-coloured jumpsuits. They were about 4½ feet (137 centimetres) high. For Herrmann, there was no question but that his experience was a 'Satanic delusion'. After that, whenever he saw a UFO – and he was to have several more encounters – he would renounce it in God's name. This apparently worked very effectively.

It is important to note that Herrmann was a fundamentalist Baptist by persuasion. Clearly, his experiences were in some way related to his beliefs. What is less clear, however, is whether his beliefs caused his experience, or whether they simply caused him to interpret it in a particular way. As a matter of historical fact, the majority of UFO reports

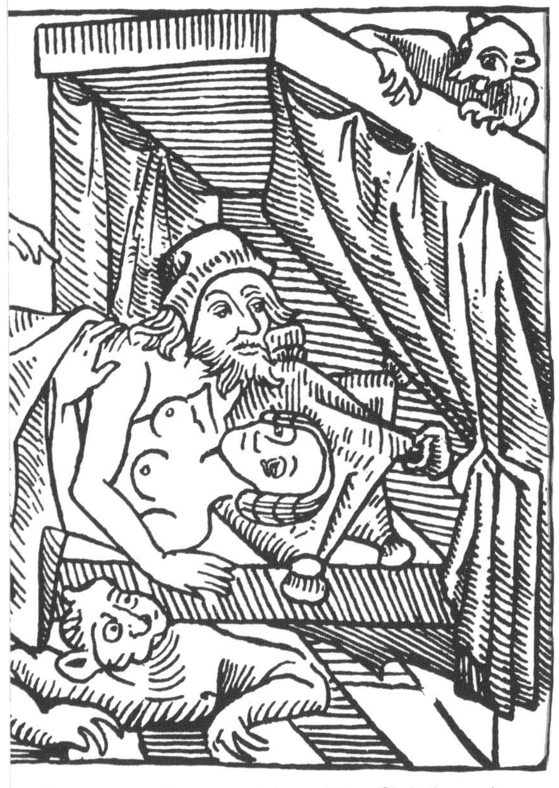

The begetting of the Antichrist, with attendant demons, is illustrated in the 15th-century woodcut, left. The existence of the Antichrist – a figure opposite to Christ in every respect – was widely given credence from the early medieval period onwards.

have come from countries with a Christian culture, so it is not surprising that most metaphysical explanations for them have a Christian slant and set the UFO in a Christian context.

Dualism Personified

There is, of course, no rigid Christian dogma concerning UFO matters; but a concept in many ways parallelling the arrival of a UFO is that of an Antichrist. Briefly, the Antichrist is a false Messiah, the exact opposite of Jesus, possessing many of his miraculous powers and offering – or seeming to offer – many of the same benefits. In fact, the origins of the idea of such a being antedate Christianity by many centuries: the notion is simply a personification of the dualism of good and evil that seems to have been one of Man's concerns since earliest times.

Over the centuries, a tradition has gradually been formulated that the Antichrist is destined to enjoy a temporary success, gaining control of Earth for a short while before a final conflict in which – it is confidently predicted – he will be worsted by Christ, who will then take over the reins of world government and inaugurate a golden age of everlasting peace. If we mere Earthlings know this, then presumably the omniscient Antichrist must know it, too; but the prospect of inevitable defeat does not seem to deter him.

Certainly, the demonic theorists have no doubt at all of the determination of the Antichrist to continue the struggle; and in the turbulence of the present age with its violence, sexual permissiveness, and decline of faith, they see all the indications that the coming of the Antichrist is at hand. Some even believe that UFOs could be the tangible signs that herald that coming. Two American theorists who take this view are John Weldon and Zola Levitt. In their book *UFOs – What on Earth is Happening?*, they state:

'UFOs are a manifestation of demon activity... here to misguide... and they are doing pretty well. They have judiciously utilised their powers through selected people to fascinate the masses, and they have widely promulgated their doctrines. They do not march through Times Square, of course, because this would reveal too much of the spiritual world. This might make people reconsider, as well, the existence of God, and the nether forces would have advertised for their enemy.'

So just how 'real' are the UFOs? Are they solid objects or subtle delusions? Weldon and Levitt ask:

'Are the flying machines really up there? Maybe so; it's not that important. If the demons wish them to be there, they are there, and if they wish people to imagine they're there, then they are imagined to be there.'

But there is no such ambiguity about the demons who pilot them:

'Are they just ideas of ours? No, not the way *The Bible* characterises them. They have motives and they take action. We are by no means making them happen or just dreaming up their activities. We believe demons can induce a whole series of experiences that, in fact, never really happened, similar to the experiences Uri Geller and Dr Puharich found were induced by their extra-terrestrial contacts. They can also, however, through various means, produce "real" UFOs which are visible

In the depiction, right, of a child being abducted by a demon, some ufologists see parallels with contemporary accounts of abductions by extra-terrestrials.

to anyone. With the powers we know demons have, they could theoretically transform a large chunk of rock into a UFO, assume human form inside of it, and land openly, thus "proving" the existence of advanced intergalactic civilisations.'

However, Weldon and Levitt doubt if this is often done. 'More likely, the standard UFO sighting is either a projection into our atmosphere, or the self-transformation of whatever material the demons themselves are composed of.' As for their purpose, Weldon and Levitt have no doubt:

'Quite simply, we think the demons are preparing the coming of the Antichrist. The Antichrist is not your run-of-the-mill world dictator. He is, in fact, something we have never contended with before; a political leader of great acumen – engaging and appealing – a kind of inverse Messiah.'

THE ALIENS WITHIN

STARTLING PARALLELS BETWEEN ABDUCTION REPORTS FROM ALL OVER THE WORLD SUGGEST THAT THESE EXPERIENCES COULD WELL BE LINKED IN SOME WAY. ACCORDING TO ONE ORIGINAL THEORY, THEY ALL STEM FROM THE VERY TRAUMA OF BEING BORN

Of all aliens reported by witnesses of close encounters of the third kind, by far most common are those of the humanoid type. Small, with disproportionately large heads and eyes, spindly-limbed, and clad in one-piece, tight-fitting suits, they often closely resemble nothing so much as a human foetus. Could this be mere coincidence – or might there be more to it?

The first striking feature is the general diminutive size of such humanoids – on average 3 – 5½ feet (90 centimetres – 1.7 metres). Humanoid reports also tell of creatures with disproportionately large heads and eyes. The foetal head size is also disproportionately large from the fourth week onwards; the eye sockets are large and, after the eyes form during the fourth week, they grow rapidly until at birth they are half the size of those of an adult – but in a body very much smaller. The bodily features of humanoids are generally reported to be rudimentary, or missing altogether. This is also true of the human foetus until very late in its development. The hands begin to form in the fifth week, and the feet in the sixth week; but fingers and toes remain webbed until around the eighth week. The underdeveloped ears, nose, mouth and shape of the face mean that the developing baby does not have a recognisably 'human' face until about the tenth week – it is, instead, very similar to what we might recognise as 'humanoid'. In most cases, humanoids are also reported as having no evident genitalia; and the genitalia of the human foetus also remain ambiguous or underdeveloped until the twelfth week.

The arms of humanoids are often described as longer than the legs; and the arms of the foetus are certainly longer than its legs until the fourth month. Humanoids walk clumsily, as if unaccustomed to such movements; the human foetus, meanwhile, does not make perceptible movements until the fifth month. Humanoids' skin is generally either pallid – grey or white – or reddish: foetal skin colour is pallid until the sixth month, and reddish in the seventh. Humanoids have wrinkled skins and hairless bodies; the human foetus has a wrinkled skin in the seventh month, and hair does not appear until the eighth month. Humanoids are often reported as having no eyebrows, and sometimes – when their skin is not wrinkled – it is said to be unnaturally smooth. Eyebrows only become visible in the unborn baby in the eighth month, and the skin becomes waxy and smooth just before birth, in the eighth and ninth months.

The similarities between humanoids reported in close encounter cases and those described in a hypnosis experiment, in which subjects were asked

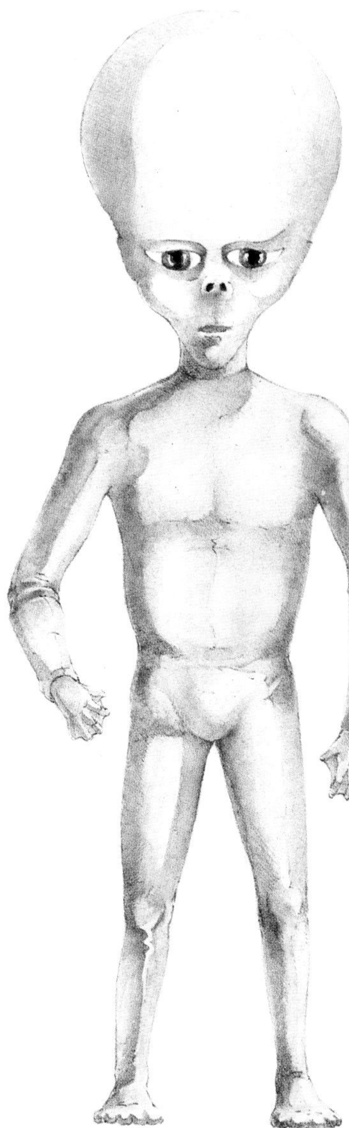

to describe an imaginary close encounter and imagery from LSD-induced 'trips', suggest that early prenatal experiences may provide a rich store of imagery that comes to the fore when triggered in some way.

Psychiatrist Stanislav Grof, with years of experience in the therapeutic use of LSD, has expressed a belief that many of his patients relive their own birth trauma during LSD sessions.

Indeed, these striking similarities suggest that the unborn child – particularly in the period of the first eight weeks from conception – may be the model for the humanoids reported in many close encounter cases.

The 10-week-old human embryo,* left, *and an artist's impression of one of the humanoids allegedly seen by Travis Walton during his five-day abduction from Heber Arizona, USA, on 5 November 1975,* below left, *bear striking similarities.

subcellular consciousness. Grof has said it is commonly reported by such subjects that they even identify with the sperm and ovum at the time of conception, and sometimes describe an accelerated process of foetal development.

One cellular component not mentioned in Grof's data, however, is potentially stunning in its implications for ufology. When the fertilised human ovum is six days old and attaches itself to the wall of the uterus, the distinctly embryonic tissue inside the ovum assumes an intriguing shape: it resembles a flattened, circular plate – the basic UFO pattern – and is then known as the embryonic disc. This stage of prenatal life is the first in which the fertilised tissues can be thought of as something integral, whole, or individual.

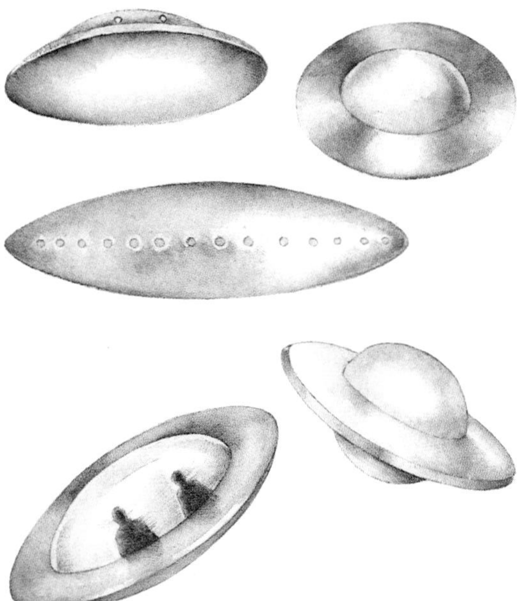

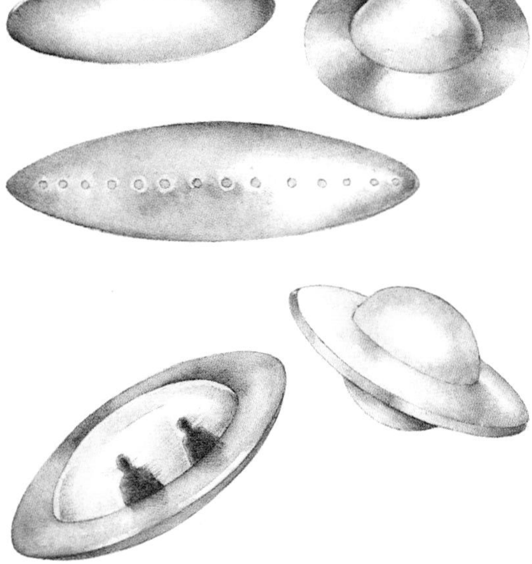

'In a way that is not quite clear at the present stage of research, the subjects' experiences seem to be related to the circumstances of the biological birth. LSD subjects frequently refer to them quite explicitly as reliving their own birth trauma. Others quite regularly show the cluster of physical symptoms that can best be interpreted as a derivative of the biological birth. They also assume postures and move in complex sequences that bear a striking similarity to those of a child during the various stages of delivery.'

Grof has also described experiences in which LSD patients seem to 'tune in' to the 'consciousness' of a particular organ or tissue of their own body, and even regress, apparently, into a cellular or

> "WITNESSES OFTEN REPORT BEING SUCKED UP IN A TUBE, APPARENTLY MADE OF LIGHT OR A LUMINOUS MATERIAL, INTO THE UFO. THESE MAY WELL BE MEMORIES OF THE BABY'S PASSAGE DOWN THE BIRTH CANAL."

It has been suggested that the travel through tunnels, frequently described in abduction reports, may well be reflections of the baby's passage down the vaginal canal, just prior to birth,* above. *The artist's impressions,* above left, *show a number of flying saucers from various UFO sightings. Six days after conception, the fertilised human egg also assumes a flattened, circular shape.

ARCHETYPAL SYMBOLS

The psychologist Carl Gustav Jung found an analogy between the shapes of 'flying saucers' and 'mandalas', which he defined as archetypal symbols of unity, wholeness, and individuation. If Grof's work is accurate, it could perhaps be interpreted as providing a physiological basis for Jung's theories about archetypal imagery and his related speculations as to the collective unconscious. At the very least, it is somewhat startling to realise that every human being who ever lived was – for a few hours – shaped very like a flying saucer. With that in mind, one can speculate that the embryonic disc may indeed manifest itself as a Jungian mandala or saucer archetype in everyone's sensibility, sometimes emerging as part of a witness's UFO-related imagery. Thus, UFO witnesses might sometimes be predisposed to perceive saucer-shaped craft in the presence of whatever psycho-physical stimulus triggers off the reaction – and what the witnesses think they perceive may be an archetypal echo of their own prenatal experiences.

One of the most difficult problems for ufology is the study of abduction cases. Often seemingly totally unsupported by reliable evidence, reports of abduction cases may seem pointless or even ridiculous; but they nevertheless present a coherent

WHO ARE THE HUMANOIDS?

MANY PEOPLE CLAIM TO HAVE MET THE OCCUPANTS OF UFOs; BUT ACCOUNTS OF HUMANOIDS' BEHAVIOUR AND APPEARANCE SEEM STRANGELY INCONSISTENT

The sighting of nine unusual flying craft in Washington State, USA, by American airman Kenneth Arnold in June 1947, marked the advent of modern publicity for the 'flying saucer' or UFO phenomenon. The frequently reported ultra-high speeds and breath-taking manoeuvrability of the objects inevitably led to speculation by observers, newsmen and the public alike that what was being witnessed were intrusions into our airspace by extra-terrestrial visitors – beings from outer space. And, as the behaviour of these objects seemed to indicate superior technology and its fluent control, the big question was: control by whom, or by what?

The question was not quickly resolved, however; for although the phenomenon was so persistent that the US Air Force set up an investigatory unit (Project Blue Book), officialdom did not appear to want to know the answer. By 1952, many accounts of sightings and even landings had been filed with the Project; but in his book *The Report on UFOs,* Blue Book's commanding officer, Captain Edward Ruppelt, stated he had been plagued by reports of landings and that his team had conscientiously ignored them.

There are, however, always those whose sense of wonder overcomes official intransigence. Groups of doggedly inquisitive civilian researchers

A purported humanoid,* above, *stands to the left of an alleged grounded UFO in the Bernina Mountains, Italy, on 31 July 1952.

The controversial picture,* above right, *shows a dead crew member from a crashed UFO found near Mexico City in the 1950s. The creature was apparently taken to Germany for examination – never to be heard of again.

drifted together and, to the limits of their slender resources, they gathered and recorded information from all around the world. Among them were people like Aimé Michel and Jacques Vallée from France (Vallée subsequently lived and worked in the USA); Coral and Jim Lorenzen and their Aerial Phenomena Research Organisation (APRO) in Arizona; Len Stringfield in Ohio; Major Donald Keyhoe's National Investigations Committee on Aerial Phenomena (NICAP) in Washington DC (who, like Ruppelt, were at first none too happy about the many landing reports) and, in Britain, the supporters of the *Flying Saucer Review.*

ALIEN PHENOMENON

From the impressive body of evidence collected by these veterans, and others, it is quite obvious now that the occupants of UFOs constitute a phenomenon in their own right. Indeed, the shapes, sizes, appearance and behaviour of these 'pilots', as reported by their alleged observers, are often quite extraordinary. Out of the thousands of reported sightings, no coherent picture emerges of their nature and intentions, however, and their actions seldom seem to be related to any kind of organised surveillance of our planet. Sometimes, sightings of these aliens are even reported without the apparent presence of a UFO.

From 1947 to 1952, while the reality of UFOs and their occupants was often the subject of heated debate, allegedly man-like creatures had already been observed either close to, or actually in, UFOs in widely different parts of the world.

Brazilian Landing

At Bauru, in the state of Sao Paulo, Brazil, on 23 July 1947, for instance, – less than a month after Kenneth Arnold's aerial encounter near Mount Rainier – a survey worker named José Higgins, and several of his fellow workers, saw a large metallic disc come to earth and settle down on curved legs.

Higgins stood his ground while his colleagues fled, and he soon found himself face to face with three 7-foot (2.1 metres) tall beings, all wearing transparent overalls with metal boxes on their backs. One entity pointed a tube at him and moved as though to apprehend him. But Higgins dodged the creature and observed that it was shy of following him into the sunlight.

The creatures had large bald heads, big round eyes, no eyebrows or beards and long legs. They leapt and gambolled, picking up and tossing huge boulders about. They also made holes in the ground, perhaps trying to indicate what could have been the positions of planets around the sun, and pointing particularly to the seventh hole from the centre. (Could that seventh 'planet' signify Uranus?) The creatures then re-entered their craft, which took off with a whistling noise. Higgins' subsequent account appeared in two Brazilian newspapers.

Three weeks later, far away in north-eastern Italy, a Professor Johannis was on a mountain walk on 14 August 1947, near Villa Santina, Carni, in the province of Friuli, when he suddenly saw a red metallic disc in a rocky cleft and emerged from trees to look at it. He then noticed that two dwarf-like creatures were following him, moving with tiny strides, hands perfectly motionless at their sides, and heads still. As they came nearer, Johannis' strength failed him: he seemed paralysed.

Captain Edward J. Ruppelt, top, was the commanding officer of the highly-criticised Project Blue Book; Aimé Michel, centre, a famous French UFO investigator; and Major Donald E. Keyhoe, the head of the National Investigations Committee on Aerial Phenomena (NICAP), based in Washington DC, USA.

***Artist's impressions of the humanoids reported by José Higgins in Brazil and Professor Johannis in Italy in 1947 are shown* left *and* top right.**

The little beings – less than 3 feet (1 metre) tall – wore translucent blue coveralls, with red collars and belts. The witness could detect no hair, but he described their facial skin colour as 'earthy green'. He also noted straight noses, slits for mouths that opened and closed like fishes' mouths, and large, round, protruding eyes.

Johannis says he shouted to them on an impulse and waved his alpine pick, whereupon one dwarf raised a hand to his belt, the centre of which apparently emitted a puff of smoke. The pick flew out of Johannis' hand, and he fell flat on his back. One entity then retrieved the pick, and the pair retreated to the disc, which soon shot up, hovered briefly over the panic-stricken professor, and then suddenly seemed to shrink and vanish.

Crash Landing

On 19 August 1949, in Death Valley, California, two prospectors saw the apparent crash-landing of a disc. Two small beings emerged and were chased by the prospectors until the aliens were lost among sand dunes. But when the two men returned to their site, the disc-shaped object had gone.

Argentine rancher Wilfredo Arévalo saw one 'aluminium' disc land while another hovered over it on 18 March 1950. The object that landed was surrounded by a greenish-blue vapour, and in its centre was a transparent cabin in which Arévalo saw 'four tall, well-shaped men dressed in Cellophane-like clothing'. They shone a beam of light at the rancher, the disc glowed a brighter blue, flames shot from the base, and it rose from the ground. The two objects then disappeared swiftly towards the Chilean border.

Such reports seemed to promise interesting material for future investigation, but did not appear to indicate a serious threat of alien ('take me to your leader') invasion. There was, too, an official reluctance even to consider landing reports, which were

APOCALYPSE NOW?

CERTAIN GROUPS OF UFO CONTACTEES OFTEN GIVE DETAILED WARNINGS OF IMPENDING DISASTERS. WHAT IS MORE, THESE CULTS INVARIABLY INSIST THAT ONLY THEIR OWN CHOSEN FEW WILL BE SAVED – A PROMISE THAT, NOT SURPRISINGLY, ATTRACTS MANY HOPEFUL DEVOTEES

Most UFO cults have appeared in the United States, long the home of countless eccentric religious groups. The story of one of these cults is told in full by a trio of sociologists, Leon Festinger, Henry Riecken and Stanley Schachter. They planted observers in a developing group centred on a UFO 'communicator' in 'Lake City', Utah. (The sociologists used fictitious names throughout in order to protect their subjects.) The communicator was 'Marian Keech', who believed she had received the initial message from her late father. She sat quietly and regularly thereafter, waiting to produce automatic writing, and was soon contacted by 'higher forces' – firstly, by 'the Elder Brother', and then by entities from the planets Clarion and Cerus (neither of which is known to conventional astronomy). She received communications especially from a certain Sananda of Clarion, who claimed to have been Jesus in an earlier time. Marian did not publicise her messages enthusiastically, but others from existing UFO groups and mystical or occult groups soon showed an interest. In August 1954, a press release was issued. This summarised not only the more philosophical part of the communications, in which the media took little interest, but also predictions regarding a coming disaster of vast proportions. The nature of the event, as reported by Marian, varied at times; but as interest in the group grew, its details became more firmly fixed. At the end of September, the *Lake City Herald* published this typical report:

'Lake City will be destroyed by a flood from Great Lake just before dawn, December 21st, according to a suburban housewife. Mrs Marian Keech of 847 West School Street says the prophecy is not her own. It is the purport of many messages she has received by automatic writing... The messages, according to Mrs Keech, are sent to her by superior beings from a planet called "Clarion".

In a still from a television science fiction play,* left, *a throng of young people, controlled by armed police, gather at an ancient stone circle in the expectation that UFOs are about to take them to a new existence beyond the Earth. At gatherings such as this, badges like those,* inset, *find a ready market. Many older and rather more staid people, however, have also expected to be contacted by UFOs and delivered from imminent cataclysm.

These beings have been visiting the Earth, she says, in what we call "flying saucers". During their visits, she says, they have observed fault lines in the Earth's crust that foretoken the deluge. Mrs Keech reports she was told the flood will spread to form an inland sea stretching from the Arctic Circle to the Gulf of Mexico.'

By now, Marian Keech was referring to a group of communicators whom she called the 'Guardians', though Sananda remained the most important. Once the media had started to publicise the group, Mrs Keech and her associates began to be afflicted by the problems that always beset UFO contactees. Increasing numbers of visitors called at her house, often when group members were present. She had explained to the group that, if they did the right thing and were gathered together, ready, at the appointed time, they would not be drowned in the forthcoming flood but would be carried away in one or more flying saucers. The extra-terrestrials could come to make contact at any time and in any way: so Mrs Keech and her group had to decide whether or not the visitors they had were extra-terrestrials, and also whether they in fact were good or evil extra-terrestrials.

The Last Days

The cult had now fallen into the classical pattern: it had a communicator, an explanation for the UFO mystery, a message of great importance, and a 'task' for its members – not so much to publicise the disaster as to prepare themselves to survive it. As the chosen date approached, the group became more outlandish. Members gave up jobs, possessions and relationships, and some took up unusual diets. All came together to await the fulfilment of their expectations. One condition of escape required by the 'Guardians' was that all metal should be removed from the participants' persons. This led to some interesting arrangements for clothing, and a lively discussion about dental fillings.

Salvation from ageing and death was promised by George van Tassel, the Sage of Giant Rock. Supposedly on instructions from extra-terrestrials, he built the structure* above, *the 'Integatron', at Giant Rock Airport in California, USA. It was intended for research into the unseen truths of life and for development of techniques of preventing and even reversing the processes of ageing in the human body. The structure, four storeys high, was made mostly of timber and contained no metal.

The last few days before 21 December were traumatic for the group members, as their hopes were first raised and then dashed by increasingly strange messages and predictions, all proving to be inaccurate. The greatest shock came on the day itself, when no flood arrived, nor any spacecraft to save them from it. The group now fell prey to disillusion and, in due course, dispersed.

Another group that purveyed warnings of catastrophe transmitted from space beings called itself the 'Light Affiliates'. They were active in the late 1960s in Burnaby, British Columbia, Canada. Their launching statement read: 'We wish to notify all those interested that a phenomenon has occurred here in Vancouver. A young girl, age 22, suddenly began channelling on 23.10.69. Her source is a being identifying himself as Ox-Ho, who is relaying transmissions from a galaxy close to our own... Her material is phenomenal in that she has been informed of the coming disasters, when to expect them, and what to do pertaining to the necessary evacuation of the danger areas and food supplies that will be needed.' The real name of the 'channel' was Robin McPherson, but she was renamed 'Estelle' by the 'being'. Her mother Aileen became 'Magdalene', her friend Sally became 'Celeste', and a young man involved in the early communications was given the evocative name 'Truman Merit'.

Ox-Ho explained that the day of judgement would begin during 22 November 1969. In these final hours, Man would be 'given a last opportunity to repair his decadent house before the terminal series of disasters'. If he did not take the opportunity to change, 'the Space Brothers would remove the Chosen and return them to Earth after the planet had once again "crystallised", and been spiritually, as well as physically, restructured.' This 'restructuring' would involve the tilting of the Earth on its axis and the disappearance beneath the sea of large land areas. Members of the 'Light Affiliates' were also exhorted to evangelise wherever possible.

Nothing seems to have happened on the predicted date to fulfil the expectations of the 'Light Affiliates'. Robin McPherson then ceased to communicate, but her mother continued the task. In an interview with the writer Brad Steiger, in the mid 1970s, she explained where the predictions had gone wrong:

'We misinterpreted them, Brad, because it all happened so suddenly. The first visions I was given of destruction were very upsetting. I can see things now in a much broader perspective... The thing is that it is the first ascension, and it is a mental ascension. The Brothers are trying to get as many people as possible into the Kingdom... You know, I've been told by the Brotherhood that Earth is like an encounter therapy centre for the psychotics of the Universe... I have been shown that the Earth is also wobbling very drastically on its axis.'

It is sometimes less painful to find ways of showing that your beliefs are fundamentally correct by means of some elaborate reinterpretation than to concede that they are simply mistaken.

Claims that intelligent beings can visit us from the planets of the solar system have been made implausible by space exploration. Alien entities must come from distant star systems, even from other galaxies, of which science presently knows little. Some UFO cults – though by no means all – have adapted to the growth of knowledge by placing the source of their communications in suitably remote places.

The group that made the greatest impact during the 1970s was called 'HIM' – Human Individual Metamorphosis. This group appeared in California in 1975 and appealed to some of those who had dabbled in the drug culture, personal spiritual development and New Age mysticism. The movement was run by a middle-aged man and woman. They adopted names that were modest enough – Bo and Peep – and their teaching offered the advantages of life after death without the inconvenience of dying. Instead, the adherents were to ascend physically.

Joan Culpepper, seen* above, *with two members of the cult, told reporters about her life with Human Individual Metamorphosis (HIM), run by a couple calling themselves Bo and Peep,* below right. *HIM offered its followers the prospect of being transported physically to a realm beyond the Earth's atmosphere. Joan Culpepper subsequently left the cult and set up a half-way house to assist other disillusioned former adherents.

One of the cult's publicity posters read:

'UFOs: why they are here. Who they have come for. When they will land. Two individuals say they were sent from the level above human and will return to that level in a spaceship within the next three months. This man and woman will discuss how the transition from the human level to the next level is accomplished, and when this may be done... If you have ever entertained the idea that there might be a real physical level in space beyond the Earth's confines, you will want to attend this meeting.'

More than Human

Bo and Peep – formerly known as M.H. Applewhite and Bonnie Nettles – had convinced themselves that they were more than human, and had the strength of will and personality to maintain that impression. Converts were clearly quite overwhelmed by them. At first, they claimed that they would one day be assassinated and then would be resurrected after three days. Later, these claims were set aside. As in other such groups, members were expected to make sacrifices – to give up their names and possessions, abandon the use of drugs, alcohol, radio and television, and not to indulge in sex, or even read books. The members generally lived in semi-permanent camps. The words of Bo and Peep, in an interview recounted by Brad Steiger, make their attitude to the family and other personal relationships clear:

'Husband and wife can take the trip at the same time – but not together. It would be impossible to become an individual if you went together on the trip... In order to leave this Earth's atmosphere, you

must go alone and overcome whatever needs you have for any other individual or thing of this Earth. Anything for which you depend on another human being or any thing on this Earth must be overcome'.

Being a member of 'HIM' was more like being a Moonie than participating in a traditional religion or even a traditional UFO cult. But the structure of the group was like that of other groups already described: there was a communicator, a message, and a task.

No one has yet ascended to another physical realm above the atmosphere. Not many people seem to have got their money back, either. It turned out that Bo and Peep had met each other in a psychiatric hospital, where she was a nurse and he was a patient. Yet plenty of people remained willing to believe them and to accept their discipline. Like so many fringe religions, it seems to have met spiritual needs that were shared by many people at that time.

Let us look, finally, at one further vision of salvation by UFOs – one that has been experienced in dreams by Sue and John Day, an English couple. They claim to have been taken on board an alien spacecraft near the village of Aveley in Essex. In their dreams, they saw a deep red Sun and a dark sphere hanging in a blood-coloured sky. Columns of weary men, women and children made their way through a devastated landscape towards the summit of a high hill. There, they waited for perhaps days, until their eyes caught the first glinting reflections from a formation of shining UFO-like craft appearing over the murky horizon, heading slowly in their direction. As they drew nearer, a number of these craft broke away and descended over the hilltop. Then they began to lower ramps. The people seemed to know that, at last, 'they' had come to take them away from the devastated planet Earth.

This series of dreams seemed to the Days to be a presentiment of a possible, but avoidable, future – a future holding disaster, but also salvation for a fortunate few through the intervention of UFOs. Quite when this event is due, however, still remains unknown.

Dragon Hill, near Uffington in Oxfordshire, below, *is one of England's most mysterious ancient sites. It was recognised by two contactees, John and Sue Day, as the scene of dreams foreshadowing some future disaster for the world. UFOs figured in the dreams, and saved a disease-ravaged remnant of the human race.*

" Certain cults have adopted the belief that the mission of UFOs is spiritual and that all physical efforts to determine the nature of UFOs must necessarily fail. While such may be the case, evidence to support it is clearly lacking. "

Robert Emenegger: UFOs – Past, Present and Future

THE VITAL KEY TO COMMUNICATING WITH ANY INTELLIGENT ALIEN RACES EXISTING IN SPACE IS LIKELY TO BE THE UNIVERSAL LANGUAGE OF MATHEMATICS, SCIENTISTS NOW SEEM TO AGREE

Many people have supposed that, even if signals that were obviously of artificial origin and therefore from intelligent beings, were picked up by a radio telescope on Earth, it would be impossible ever to enter into communication with alien species. How could we understand a language that no human being had ever spoken?

SIGNALS THROUGH SPACE

There are even some languages on Earth, still surviving in inscriptions, that no one understands. But it should be possible to solve the problem using basic mathematical and scientific facts.

The first task would be to design a radio message that was obviously artificial. A radio telescope can be used not only as a receiver but also as a transmitter. Thus the radio dish at Arecibo, Puerto Rico, has been used not only to pick up faint signals from distant radio sources in the heavens but also as a radar instrument, sending out powerful pulses of radiation to bounce off the planet Venus. In this way, rough maps of the solid surface of Venus were constructed even before a radar mapping instrument was put into orbit about the planet.

Suppose we used a powerful radio telescope to send out the following sequence of pulses: one pulse, gap, two pulses, gap, three pulses, gap, four pulses, gap, longer gap, six pulses. Suppose we then repeated this signal after an even longer gap and kept on doing this. Now it does not matter where in the Universe an intelligent species lives or what it is like: if it is to be regarded as intelligent, it is presumably capable of counting. And it does not

Hundreds of massed radio telescope dishes make up the proposed Cyclops system, as shown* left. *Equivalent to a single huge instrument, the array would be enormously sensitive and capable of locating the direction of a radio source with high accuracy. Cyclops could perform the most thorough search yet for weak signals from intelligences in space. First steps have been made with conventional radio telescopes, such as the instruments,* below left, *at Green Bank, West Virginia, USA. Messages have also been sent into space, though there is no hope of receiving an answer for millennia.

matter what its number scale is. Regardless of whether this consists only of one and zero, as does an electronic computer's, or contains 60 different numbers, like that of an ancient Babylonian, it will know that two is one more than one, that three is one more than two, and so on. It will realise that the signal it is picking up is simply the sequence of the first few numbers: one, two, three, four, . . ., six. It will recognise that this is an attempt to send out an obviously artificial signal, in the hope that if it is picked up by an intelligent race, it will send it back with the missing five inserted to show that the message has been understood. In order to ram home the artificiality of such a message, it could be varied from time to time with other sequences of numbers, perhaps bearing some arithmetical relationship.

Suppose now that an alien race has been contacted in this way and that they have replied, sending back the message with the missing set of pulses filled in, thus showing that they are interested in communicating. Could there be any wothwhile future in such a dialogue?

The problem would be to establish a common vocabulary of radio signals and gradually build up the number of 'words' until both races are proficient in the common 'language'. First steps would involve the transmission of simple sums.

It would be impossibly cumbersome to continue to transmit numbers in the form of simple sequences of pulses, of course. But we could easily teach the aliens our way of writing numbers more compactly in the decimal, or ten-based, system. A sequence of, say, six pulses could be transmitted, followed by a more compact signal pattern: this would correspond to showing a child a sequence of six pencil strokes followed by the written digit 6 in the course of teaching him the digits 0 to 9. When the aliens had learned the ten digits, we could send further sequences that would show how ten is represented as 10, eleven as 11, and so on.

We might then graduate to multiplications and divisions, sending such sums until the aliens realised that certain radio signals stood for the multiplication sign and the division sign. A little later, we could make it clear what symbols we were using for the ideas 'is greater than' and 'is less than'. Proceeding in this way, it is certain that an extensive set of mathematical symbols could be learned and used.

It might be thought that little progress could be made after this stage, but that is not the case. In the translation and understanding of ancient Egyptian hieroglyphics, a major breakthrough was achieved when the Rosetta Stone was discovered. This was a slab on which a single message was

InFocus

IN BLACK AND WHITE

```
0 0 0 0 1 1 1 0 0 0 0 0 0 0 1 1 1 1 1 0 0 0 0 0 0 1 0 1 0
                                                        1
0 0 0 0 0 0 0 0 0 1 0 0 0 0 0 0 0 0 0 1 0 1 0 0 0 0 0 0 0 1 1 1 1 1 0 0 0 0 0 0
1
1 1 0 0 0 0 0 0 1 1 1 1 1 1 1 0 0 0 1 1 1 1 1 1 1 1 1 0 0 1 0 1 1 1 1 1 0 1 0 0
                                                                              1
0 1 1 1 1 1 0 1 0 0 1 0 1 1 1 1 1 0 1 0 0 1 0 1 1 1 1 1 0 1 0 0 1 0 1 1 1 1 1 0
1
0 0 1 0 1 1 1 1 1 0 1 0 0 1 0 1 1 0 1 1 0 1 0 0 0 0 1 1 0 1 1 0 0 0 0 0 0 1 1 0
                                                                              1
0 0 0 0 0 0 1 1 0 1 1 0 0 0 0 0 0 1 1 0 1 1 0 0 0 0 0 0 1 1 0 1 1 0 0 0 0 0 0 1
1
1 0 1 1 0 0 0 0 0 1 1 1 0 1 1 1 0 0
```

A television picture could be transmitted to intelligent extra-terrestrials in binary code, as demonstrated *right*. Each symbol represents a single pixel (picture cell) — 0 for a white pixel, 1 for a black pixel. But how could we convey to listeners that we intend the sequence of digits to be interpreted as a television picture? A strong hint could be given by sending, say, 253 such symbols. Mathematically-inclined aliens would notice that this number is equal to 11 x 23 and that there are no other numbers that can be multiplied together to form it. This might suggest to them that the numbers refer to an array either of 23 columns of 11 elements, or to 11 columns of 23 elements. If they then tried to assemble the picture in the first of these ways, they would get a 'scrambled' result, as shown *right*. But when they tried it the other way, they would get the picture, *far right;* and if we were lucky, it would be intelligible to them.

Just such a message has already been beamed into space by the giant radio dish at Arecibo, and aimed at a tightly packed cluster of stars called M13. It therefore has a good chance of passing through a large number of planetary systems. A sequence of 1,679 digits was sent: this could be turned only into a 23 x 73 array, in which there was room for a wealth of information. The atomic numbers of five elements important to life – oxygen, nitrogen, carbon, phosphorus and hydrogen – were given. Then formulae followed, showing how these are built up into DNA, the genetic material that governs our heredity. A small humanoid figure was included, too. Scientists who did not know the code proved able to 'crack' it – which encourages the hope that aliens might, too. Unfortunately, however, any reply from M13 will reach us no sooner than AD 50,000, because the cluster is at an immense distance.

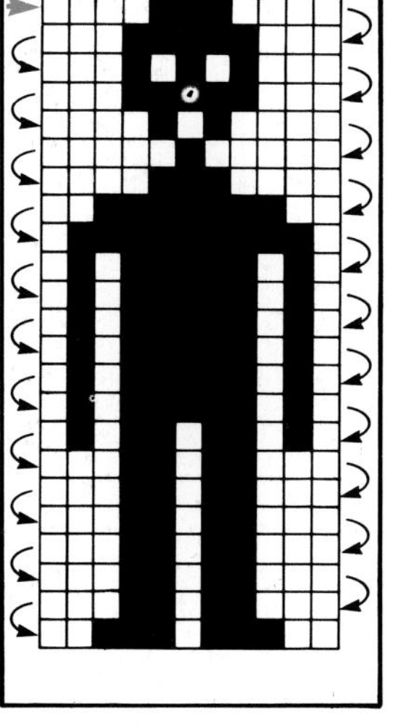

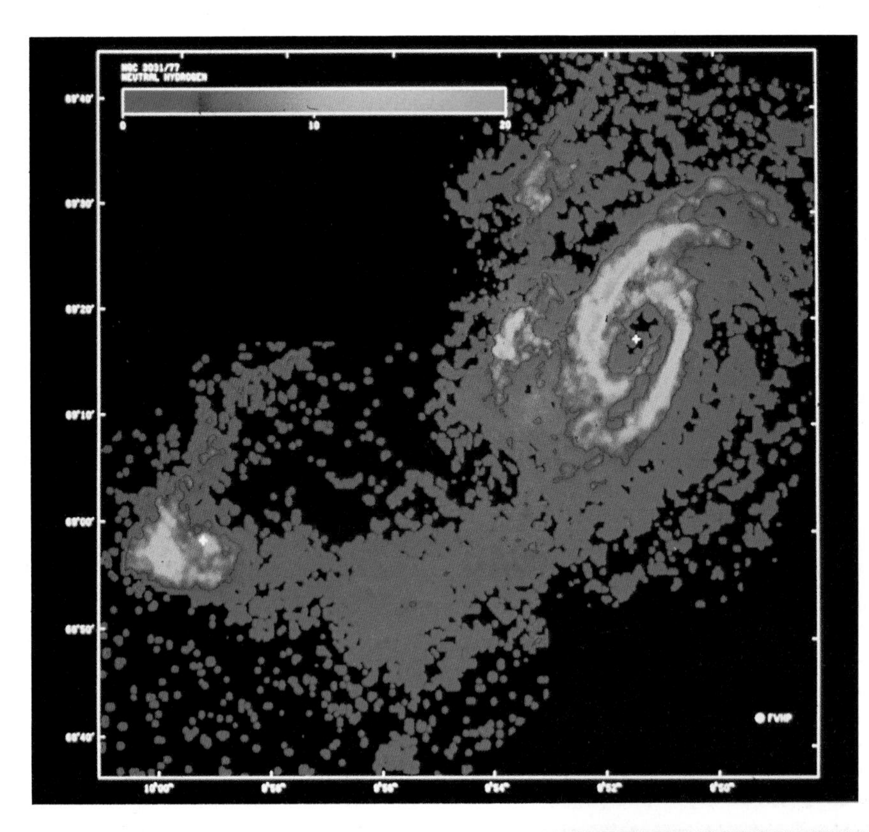

that the next thing to do would be to send out, suitably coded, the *Encyclopaedia Britannica,* thus presenting our alien friends with a comprehensive picture of Earth's civilisations. It would then probably only be a matter of time and patience before the ability to speak to each other had been achieved. From then on, progress would be limited only by the speed of radio.

For all but the nearest planetary systems, where the time between question and answer is much less than a century, interstellar conversations, however, would be between human race and alien race – not between individuals. One generation would ask its questions and hope that its descendants would think the answers worth having. For at least a percentage of questions, this would certainly be so. Aliens with other histories, and perhaps with other senses, would surely have perspectives on this mysterious Universe worth sharing. But another astronomical fact of life is the age of the Universe and our late arrival on the scene, making it probable that we are among the most primitive forms of intelligent life, with little to barter in exchange for information. To know that the human race is not alone in a huge Universe, however, would certainly remove the numbing suspicion that life on Earth is merely a highly improbable and purely temporary episode in the Universe's career.

engraved in three scripts: Egyptian hieroglyphics, Egyptian demotic script and ancient Greek. It was possible to match the Greek words with the Egyptian symbols, and from then on progress in deciphering ancient Egyptian inscriptions was rapid. The problem in enlarging our vocabulary of 'Extra-terrestrial' is to find one or more 'Rosetta Stones', that our alien friends also possess. Not only that, when we transmit our 'Rosetta Stones', the aliens must recognise what they are. There are several such 'Stones' which we might expect to be meaningful to any race that has reached our level of scientific and technological civilisation.

One of these is the periodic table of the elements. An astronomical fact of life, the sameness of the Universe, tells us that no matter where you go in the Universe, you find that all objects are made up of the same elements and in much the same relative proportions by mass.

The table of elements is a vast body of nuclear, chemical, electrical and numerical information. It can be used to define natural units for distance, mass, electrical charge and time; and with its aid, we should be able to teach the aliens our words 'hydrogen', 'helium', 'carbon', 'electron', 'proton', 'neutron' and so on. By sending symbolic descriptions of chemical reactions, we would be presenting our correspondents with easily understood lessons in our language. By this time, in addition, the mutual understanding of mathematics would also enable pictures to be sent in much the same way that thousands of pictures of Jupiter and Saturn were sent back to Earth from the Voyager spacecraft – namely, in digital form. The signal would consist of a stream of numbers, representing information about the brightness and colour of the picture at each point.

At international conferences devoted to the search for extra-terrestrial life, it is often suggested

Two galaxies 'seen' at a radio wavelength of 21 centimetres, are shown top. Clouds of hydrogen in space emit radio noise at this wavelength on which aliens messages may well be broadcast.

The surface of Venus as revealed by radar carried in a space probe is shown above. The radar data came to Earth as a string of numbers. The same principle could, of course, be used to send pictures to aliens.

ILKLEY MOOR ENTITY

Of all the cases reported to UFO researcher Peter Hough, none has generated as much interest as the alleged abduction by an alien of a former police officer on Yorkshire's Ilkley Moor

***The mysterious alien, as photographed by Philip Spencer, is circled in the shot* above.**

Philip Spencer had left his house at approximately 7.10 a.m. on 1 December 1987, for a four-mile trek across Ilkley Moor in order to visit his father-in-law in the village of East Morton, Yorkshire. He took with him a compass and a cheap 35mm camera, loaded with 400 Kodak film, to take some shots of Ilkley from the moor tops. Spencer had taken the walk two or three times previously in the four months since he and his wife had moved into the area, but he always took the compass 'for safety'.

Half-an-hour later, in an area of the moor known as White Wells, a movement to his right caught Spencer's attention. He looked around, and ten feet (3 metres) away stood a strange green creature. It was, he says, about 4 feet 6 inches tall (1.37 metres), with spindly arms and legs, sausage-thick fingers, a slit of a mouth, no discernible nose, large dark eyes and long ears.

In the time it took to bring up his camera, however, the entity had scuttled away. It then turned, making a dismissive gesture with its right arm, at which point Spencer managed to click the shutter. He tried to chase the creature around a buff, but when he got there, it had gone. Hovering nearby, though, was a silver saucer-shaped object which immediately shot upwards, promptly disappearing into cloud.

Rather taken aback, the young man returned home, only to discover that it was 10 a.m., and not 8.15 a.m., as he expected. How had he lost almost two hours of his life? Spencer feared for his sanity, and caught a bus to the nearby town of Keighley, where there was a film-processing company with a one-hour service. The resultant print was underexposed with a degree of camera shake; nevertheless, the image of a 'green creature' confirmed he was not going mad.

Philip's wife, knowing her husband to be a truthful person, was equally bemused at what she saw. The whole thing seemed absurd. What was more, the polarity of Spencer's compass was now entirely reversed. He clearly needed to contact someone who had experience in these matters, and found an address for Jenny Randles, a leading UFO investigator who, together with Arthur Tomlinson and myself, arranged to meet with him.

We visited the site, and noticed a deep indentation in the ground, where Spencer had seen the hovering disc-shaped object. Our next step was to examine the photographic evidence, and the negative was given to three independent analysts. There was, it seemed, more to the photograph than at first apparent, for to the right of the creature was a box-like image situated above the outcropping, and in exactly the same place that Philip allegedly came across the silver disc. Was this 'blob' in the picture the 'box' on top of the spacecraft? Researchers from the *Independent UFO Network* took some pictures at the same place as Spencer, and one of them showed up a 'blob', too. But this was thought to be a light reflection off the opposite bank, which showed up only if the lighting conditions and moisture content of the ground were exactly right. It should be made clear that at no time did Philip Spencer claim the 'blob' was the 'box'. The speculation was entirely mine.

> " IF THE PHOTOGRAPH DOES INDEED DEPICT A UFO ENTITY, THEN IT TAKES THE WHOLE ABDUCTION QUESTION AWAY FROM THE REALMS OF SOCIAL AND PSYCHOLOGICAL THEORY, AND INTO A MORE FRIGHTENING SCENARIO OF PHYSICAL REALITY. "

It is, of course, necessary to take a critical look at Spencer's claims. After all, this was a most extraordinary case – there have been groups of debunkers in the past who have set out deliberately to make false claims in order to discredit investigators at a later date. But Philip Spencer did not fit the bill of a lone hoaxer. He would not allow himself to be photographed, and the last thing he wanted was to see his name in lights. Neither did he seek to get any money from the case.

A week after the photographic analysis, Philip called and asked about the possibility of hypnosis, as he felt that this might help him to regain his memory of the missing time. We arranged for a clinical psychologist, Jim Singleton, to interview the witness and carry out hypnotic regression. What emerged under hypnosis was even more amazing than the story Philip had already told us.

In long, drawn out sentences, Philip described walking up the hillside and suddenly becoming paralysed as the creature approached him. Then he found himself in a brightly-lit room, and placed on a table where he underwent some sort of examination by four or five of the creatures. He then found himself back on the moors with no memory of the abduction, and one-and-three-quarter hours missing from his life. It is at this point, at the end of the experience, that the picture was taken.

Of course, hypnosis is no truth-drug, although it has been used by the police in order to ascertain details of car number plates or the physical description of assailants. Jim Singleton thought Spencer's experience 'very consistent', especially as he had material evidence to back it up.

In May 1989, at my request, Spencer agreed to help in a reconstruction for NIPPON television, who were making a documentary. The company blacked out his face and disguised his voice to ensure anonymity. Philip made it plain from the start he would accept no fee, and it was only with persuasion that he took his expenses. During the intervening years, Philip has impressed me with his honesty, but as a serious ufologist, I feel I have to suspend judgment on this very unusual and important case.

If the photograph does indeed depict a UFO entity, then it takes the whole abduction question away from the realms of social and psychological theory, and into a more frightening scenario of physical reality.

A LOGIC OF THEIR OWN

TWO TERRIFYING INCIDENTS FROM JAPAN, TOGETHER WITH ONE FROM ITALY, OFFER INTRIGUING CLUES ABOUT UFO POWER

One of the most curious categories to be found in files of reported UFO sightings consists of isolated reports of UFOs landing on rivers or lakes and siphoning up considerable quantities of water. We report on two cases, widely separated in both space and time: the first is from Japan; the second, from northern Italy in 1952. In both instances, the amount of water taken on board by the UFOs suggests that it was not intended merely for scientific analysis – yet what else was it for? Are we to believe that UFOs are powered or cooled by water, or that their occupants need water for drinking or cooking? A third case is one of the weirdest ever to have been reported in Japan. Yet no UFO was observed during the incident.

If some alien entities can survive without spacecraft, why are others so apparently vulnerable that they require regular supplies of water? Reports simply do no add up to a coherent picture of the perplexing phenomenon.

The artists' impressions, **below** *and* **above opposite,** *are of a close encounter at Tomakomai, Hokkaido, Japan, in July 1973.*

Some years ago, *Flying Saucer Review* received an exciting account of one of the occasional sightings of UFOs taking on water. It came from a Japanese UFO investigator, Jun-Ichi Takanashi of Osaka. Shadowy humanoid beings were also said to have been observed. The event took place at Tomakomai, a small industrial town on the southern coast of Hokkaido, the northernmost island of Japan, in July 1973. The eyewitness was Masaaki Kudou, a university student, then aged 20. He was home on vacation, and had taken a temporary job as a night security guard at a timber yard.

After patrolling the premises in his car, Kudou returned to the prescribed place from which he could observe the premises – as well as the waters of the bay beyond – and settled back to listen to his radio, light a cigarette, and relax. It was a still night, with the stars clearly visible. Suddenly he saw a streak of light flash across the sky, a spectacular 'shooting star' that suddenly stopped in its tracks, vanished, and reappeared. Remaining stationary, the light now expanded and contracted alternately at high speed, growing until it reached the apparent size of a baseball held at arm's length. It darted about and Kudou found himself dizzily trying to follow its gyrations. Then, as it began to descend towards the sea, the young student felt a surge of alarm, especially when the light halted near a distant cement works, and began to direct a beam of intermittent pulses of green light towards the north.

> AROUND HIS CAR, EVERYTHING WAS LIT UP AS THOUGH BY DAYLIGHT, AND HE SAW WHAT APPEARED TO BE WINDOWS AROUND THE DIAMETER OF THE SPHERICAL OBJECT. IN THE MIDDLE OF ONE OF THESE, THERE WAS A SHADOWY HUMAN-SHAPED FIGURE.

Next, the object continued its descent towards the sea, this time sweeping in an arc until it was in a position much closer to the student observer. It halted its descent at about 70 feet (20 metres) from the sea, and the student was amazed to see a transparent tube emerge and lower itself towards the water. A soft *min-min-min-min* noise could be heard as this was happening, and the pitch of the noise lowered as the tube descended. When the tube touched the water, its lower edge glowed, and it seemed that water was being sucked up into the object above.

Masaaki Kudou wondered if he was dreaming or if his imagination was playing tricks with him. He lowered his gaze for a minute or so; and when he looked up once again, the water-suction operation seemed to be over, as the tube had been withdrawn from the water. No sooner had he registered this fact than the hovering UFO began to move menacingly towards him. He feared he was about to be attacked in some way, and probably killed.

The object moved into a position some 160 feet (50 metres) above Kudou's car. By leaning forwards and looking up, he could keep it in view. He says its surface was as smooth as a table-tennis ball and, emitting its own glow, appeared to be white. Around his car, everything was lit up as though by daylight, and he saw what appeared to be windows around the diameter of the spherical object. In the middle of one of these, there was a shadowy human-shaped figure, while to the right there were two smaller shapes in another of the windows, but Kudou could not see whether or not these were similar to the first. All this, plus a sudden feeling that he was bound hand and foot, was too much for the witness, who began to rock his head in his hands, with his chin on the steering wheel, moaning to himself.

Nevertheless, Kudou still felt an urge to look upwards and, straining to do this, he saw in the sky above the car three or four newly-arrived glowing objects, similar in all respects to the first one. There was also a large, dark brown object, in silhouette, which he said looked like 'three gasoline drums connected together lengthwise' and which hovered noiselessly.

Suddenly the whole phenomenal spectacle came to an end. The glowing spheres swiftly manoeuvred into position and disappeared into one end of the large 'gasoline can' objects. This in turn shot off to the north, rather like a shooting star. The witness sat motionless, numb all over. He slowly became aware that his car radio was giving forth meaningless sounds, and that he himself was suffering from a severe headache. He was later able to estimate that the whole terrifying incident had lasted for only about 12 minutes in all.

WATER-SAMPLING

Another incident involving water occurred at 3 a.m. on 25 July 1952, when a keen fisherman named Carlo Rossi was walking alongside the River Serchio, opposite San Pietro a Vico in Lucca, northern Italy. Puzzled by the appearance of an unusual light from an unseen position on the river below, he climbed the high embankment, and looked down to see a huge circular craft with a transparent cupola on top, and a shallow turret underneath from which three legs protruded, supporting the body of the craft above the water. There was also a ladder, and a long tube by which, apparently, the craft was taking in water. Suddenly, a port opened in the upper part of the turret, and Carlo saw a 'human' figure look out. This figure pointed at the fisherman, who scrambled down the embankment. A green ray passed over his head, and he threw himself down. Looking up, seconds later, he saw the craft rise above the embankment and move off at high speed towards Viareggio.

The illustration, **below,** ***depicts another close encounter of the third kind, at Lucca, Italy, on 25 July 1952.***

Rossi was badly shaken by the incident but something that happened a few weeks later worried him much more. To the outsider, the incident seems trivial – although it is a classic example of a 'man in black' encounter: a strange man approached Rossi and offered him, Rossi said, a 'bad' cigarette. Rossi was terrified. He used later to say: 'I wonder if they want to do me harm, maybe, because of the thing I saw in the river?'

The circumstances of Rossi's subsequent death seem to lend substance to his suspicion. He was riding home on his bicycle one day when he was knocked down by a car. The driver, however, was never identified.

Other aliens, however, seem to show no interest in water, but the purpose behind their actions can be just as mysterious. One particularly alarming experience occurred on the evening of 3 October 1978, when Hideichi Amano, using his mobile unit

Hideichi Amano,* right, *victim of the Sayama encounter, recounted his experience on a television programme.
***An artist's impression of the strange humanoid creature seen by Mr Amano, is shown* below.**

radio car, drove up a mountain outside Sayama City, Japan, at about 8.30 p.m. with his two-year-old daughter, Juri. Amano, who owned a snack bar and was also a keen radio ham, made the trip so that he could get unrestricted radio transmission and reception for a conversation with his brother, who lived in a distant part of the country. When their hook-up was finished, and a few other local calls had been made, Amano was about to drive back down the mountain when the interior of the car suddenly became very bright. A light ten times brighter than normal was coming from the fluorescent tube he had fitted inside the car. He observed that this light was confined to the car's interior: none, he said, was passing through the windows. Moments earlier, Juri had been standing on the passenger seat beside him, but now her father was aghast to see the child lying on the seat and foaming at the mouth. At the same instant, he became aware of a round patch of orange light that was beamed through the windscreen and on to his stomach, and he saw that this was coming from a point in the sky. Then his alarm turned to terror when he sensed something metallic being pressed against his right temple.

Amano glanced sideways and saw an unearthly humanoid creature standing there with a pipe-like device in its mouth, and it was this that was being pressed against Amano's head. From the tube came an incessant babble, as if from a tape being played too fast. Was the humanoid somehow reading Amano's brain waves, or perhaps acquiring a form of electrical power in this way?

The witness said the creature had a round face, but no neck, two sharply pointed ears, two small, motionless eyes that glowed bluish-white, and a triangular depression on its forehead. The mouth was clamped round the pipe, and no nose could be seen. While the babble continued, Amano says he found it difficult to move, and his mind became strangely 'vague'.

The terrified radio ham tried to start the car to flee the place, but there was no response from the

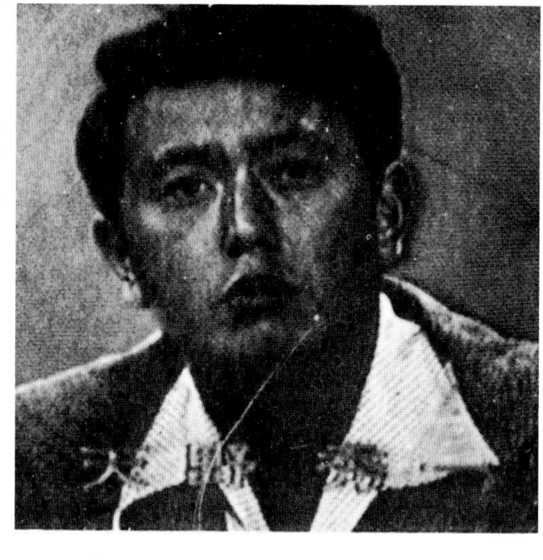

engine, and the lights would not work either. Then, after four or five minutes, the creature began to fade and slowly vanished. The orange light disappeared, the interior lighting returned to normal, and other equipment that had previously been switched on now began to function again. When the headlights returned, Amano switched on the starter and got an instant response. Still in a confused state, he roared away down the hill, and it was only when he reached the lower slopes that he remembered little Juri's condition. As he stopped, however, the child stood up and said: 'I want a drink of water, papa.'

" THE WITNESS SAID THE CREATURE HAD A ROUND FACE ... AND A TRIANGULAR DEPRESSION ON ITS FOREHEAD. WHILE THE BABBLE CONTINUED, AMANO FOUND IT DIFFICULT TO MOVE. 

The witness decided to report the experience to the police, but they only poked fun at him, so he went home and retired to bed, still suffering from a severe headache.

Researchers for a television programme heard of the affair and eventually arranged for Amano to be questioned under hypnosis in front of the cameras. One piece of information retrieved was that the creature was alleged to have told him to return to the meeting place at a certain time. To avoid a stampede by the curious, this was not revealed to viewers.

Investigator Jun-Ichi Takanashi, however, seemed to have little faith in the regression session because the 'hypnotist's insistence on more information was far too severe'. He even suspected that the idea of a second meeting with the humanoid was a creation of the witness's subconscious mind. The fact that no second meeting was ever reported seems to lend weight to this. Yet, despite his reservations, Takanashi considered the encounter, as originally reported, to be 'the strangest ever to have taken place in Japan'.

TWO ELECTRIFYING EXPERIENCES

IN THE SPACE OF A WEEK, TWO COUNTRY LANES WERE SCENES OF TERRIFYING CLOSE ENCOUNTERS. WERE THEY PART OF A PLANNED ATTACK?

The blue light in the sky, **right,** *was seen by motor-cyclist Paul Green as he approached Langenhoe Hall, in Essex. It was emitting a strange, high-pitched humming noise.*

One of the curiosities of the history of UFOs is clustering activity, in which several incidents occur within a small locality only a few days apart. Sometimes the events are similar; sometimes – as in the following close encounters in south-east England – they appear to be linked only by place and time. But always there is a strange inconclusiveness about them, something that suggests that, if only we could find the missing link, we would understand what it is that those behind the UFO phenomenon are trying to tell us.

The first event occurred on a Sunday morning, 14 September 1965, at about one o'clock. An engineer named Paul Green, aged 29, was riding his motorcycle in a southwardly direction along the B1025 road, which runs between Colchester and West Mersea in Essex. He had been visiting his fiancée, and was now on his way home. The motorcycle was going well, purring along at some 40 miles per hour (70 km/hr).

He had just passed through the village of Langenhoe, and was up to Pete Tye Common, where he overtook a rider on a motor scooter. A minute or so later, he was approaching Langenhoe Hall when he suddenly heard a high-pitched humming noise away to his left – in the east. As the noise became louder, he looked up, expecting to see an approaching aeroplane, but he saw only a small point of blue light that was about 5 miles (8 kilometres) away to the east, approximately over the town of Brightlingsea.

As Paul Green watched the light winking, and then growing brighter and flashing, he realised that it was moving in his direction. Rapidly it became larger, and at the same time the humming that he had become aware of became louder and louder, too. Once the object was over Langenhoe Marsh, Paul became uneasily aware that his motorcycle engine was now coughing and spluttering, and after it had 'missed' several times, it suddenly stopped dead and the lights went off.

At that point, the flashing blue light was just over a mile (just under 2 kilometres) away, to the east of the road. Watching intently, Paul now saw, within the extreme brightness of the light, an enormous object that resembled the upper half of a large spinning top. It was about as big as a gasometer, with a dome on the upper part. Fierce blue flashes of light apparently emanated from inside this dome. By now, the object had stopped moving in Paul's direction and, instead, was descending slowly; at one stage, it tilted its underside towards him. The outer rim of the craft carried a number of round objects spaced equidistantly, so that it gave the impression of what he described as a 'luminous ball-race'.

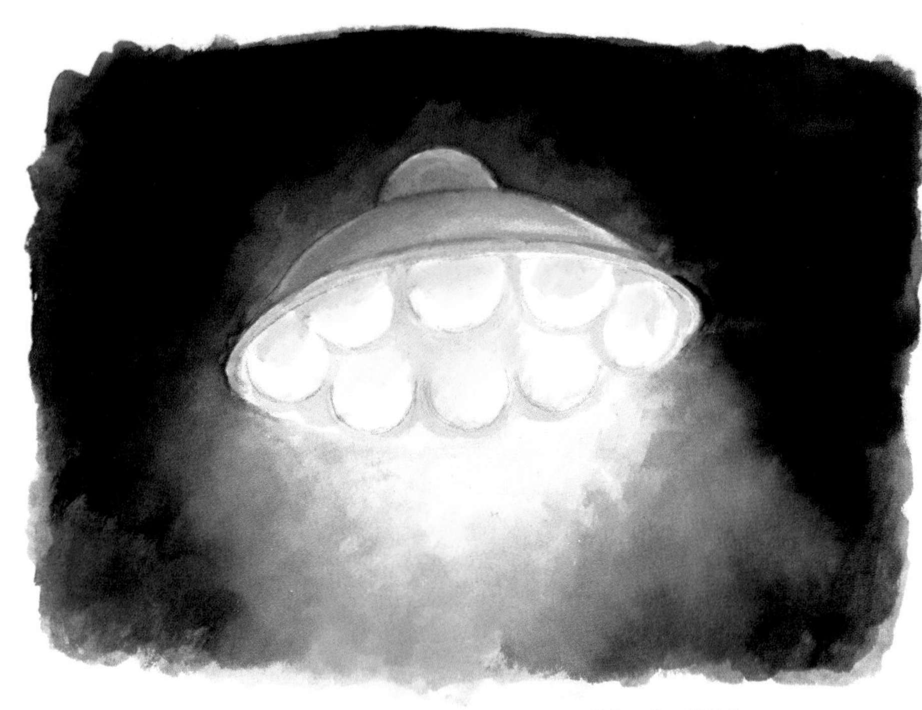

Paul Green dismounted from his motorcycle and took a few involuntary steps towards the object, quickly coming to an unsteady halt. He later said: 'I felt spellbound and unable to move or speak, just as if I had become paralysed. The flashing blue light became so intense that it was painful, and it appeared to fluctuate in rhythm with my heart beat and hit against my chest. I felt myself tingling all over, rather like the electric shock one gets when handling an electrified cattle fence.'

At last the humming died down and the UFO descended towards the farmhouses at Wick. It was about then that the scooter that Paul had overtaken also came coughing and spluttering to a halt. The rider, a young lad in a leather jacket, dismounted and stood looking at the flashing light, as if transfixed. But Paul had no time to speak to him.

Paul reported: 'My head began to throb, and felt as though there were a band tightening around it. With a great effort, I made myself move, and I grasped the bike and tried to start it.' In the end, he managed to push it along, finally achieving a bump-start. He mounted and drove home as quickly as he could. After a short distance, a line of tall hedges hid the 'thing' from him, but he could still see the blue glow in the sky.

It was unfortunate that the witness was so terrified by his encounter and the painful physiological effects that he never thought of speaking to the young man on the scooter, so that a chance of obtaining corroborative evidence was missed.

Paul Green arrived home at 2 a.m., and took the unusual course of awakening his invalid mother – he needed to tell someone of his experience. The next day, his hair and clothes were so charged with static electricity that they crackled continually.

Two weeks after his frightening experience, Paul Green was interviewed for *Flying Saucer Review* by Dr Bernard Finch, one of its regular investigators. Dr Finch was convinced that Paul's story was true, and added that: 'He described symptoms which can only be ascribed to the effects of a very powerful magnetic field on the

"WATCHING INTENTLY, PAUL NOW SAW, WITHIN THE EXTREME BRIGHTNESS OF THE LIGHT, AN ENORMOUS OBJECT THAT RESEMBLED THE UPPER HALF OF A LARGE SPINNING TOP. IT WAS ABOUT AS BIG AS A GASOMETER – WITH A DOME ON THE UPPER PART."

When the UFO flew nearer, as seen in the artist's impression* above, *Paul Green noticed that fierce blue flashes came from inside the dome on top. Under the craft were luminous, ball-like objects.
The map* below *shows Paul Green's route and the path of the UFO near West Mersea in Essex.

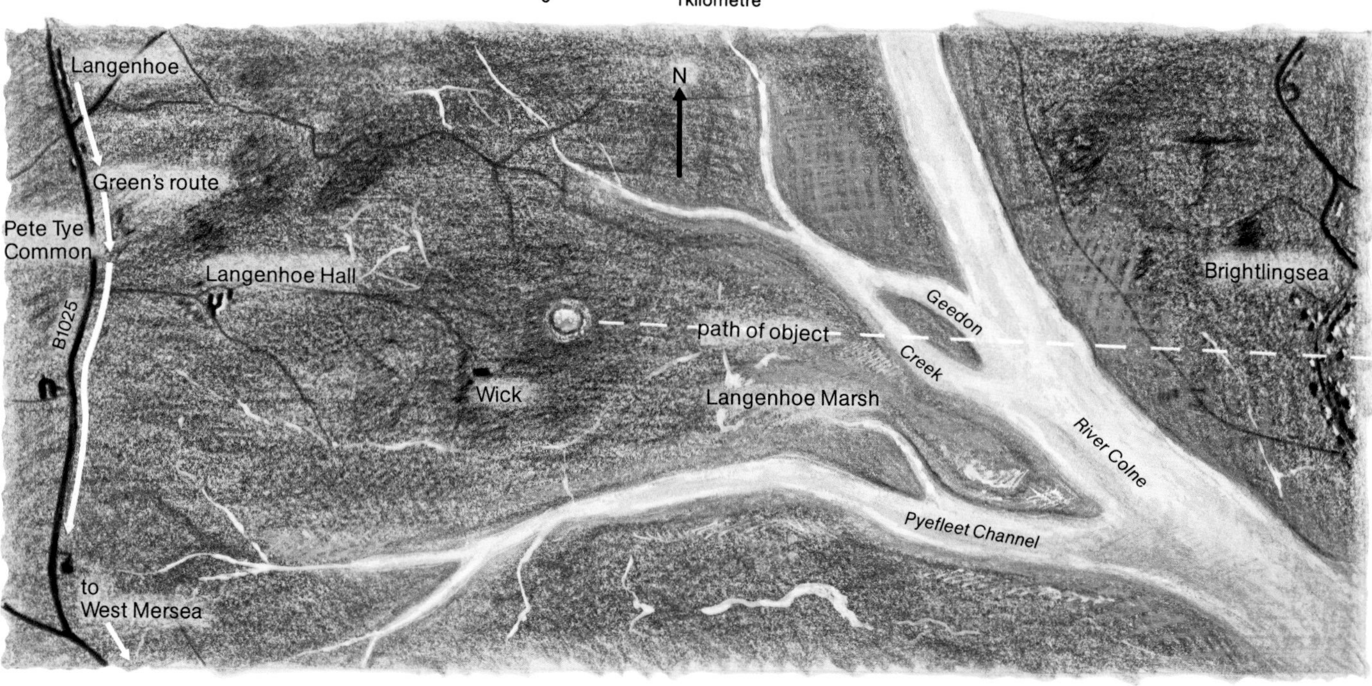

human body.' He went on to speculate that, if this field were strong enough, it could produce a kind of light 'as yet unknown to our science'.

There is an interesting postscript to the story. A few days after the incident, Paul was discussing his experience with a friend who lived at nearby Shrub End, some 5 miles (8 kilometres) north-west of Langenhoe. He told Paul that, around the time Paul saw the UFO, he was at home when suddenly his dog started to bark. He opened the door to let the dog out, and saw a large blue light passing rapidly by in the sky directly overhead, travelling towards the north-west.

Six days later, and about 20 miles (30 kilometres) from the scene of the Langenhoe close encounter of the second kind, another strange incident was reported. It may well have been a close encounter of the third kind.

Geoffrey Maskey, aged 25, had stopped his car in a Felixstowe lane known as Walton Avenue. With him were two friends, Michael Johnson and Mavis Fordyce. It was 10.30 p.m. when, without saying a word, Michael suddenly opened his door, got out and disappeared into the night. After a few minutes, the waiting friends heard a high-pitched humming noise.

Mavis was alarmed, and Geoff looked out of the car window to try to spot the source of the noise. He saw a glowing, orange-coloured, oval-shaped object some 6 feet (2 metres) in length, and about 100 feet (30 metres) above the lane. The orange glow lit up everything nearby.

The man in the flames who was seen pointing, illustrated in the sketch **right**, *was supposedly encountered by driver Geoffrey Maskey in Felixstowe, Essex.*

After the driver of the car – illustrated **below** *– had mysteriously left his vehicle, an orange, oval object was seen in the sky overhead, throwing an orange glow over everything.*

The object then disappeared behind trees, with the humming noise still sounding. Geoff called Michael's name and, when there was no response, reversed along the lane and called again. Suddenly, Michael came stumbling through a hedge, clutching his neck and his eyes. The others thought he was playing a game with them, until he collapsed in the road. Geoff went over to him and found he was unconscious. They got him into the car and took him to Felixstowe Hospital.

Michael regained consciousness at the hospital. The doctor diagnosed severe shock. There were also burn marks on the back of his neck, and a bump below his right ear. As a precaution, Michael was transferred to Ipswich Hospital, and Geoff Maskey was not allowed to see him again until he was discharged, next afternoon. Michael spoke then about a force that seemed to pull him from the car, and of 'a man in the flames pointing at him.'

The remarkable thing was that, if indeed there had been 'a force' capable of pulling a man from a car (or, more likely, a mental compulsion to leave the car), then it was certainly selective; neither Mavis nor Geoff felt its influence in any way.

The *Ipswich Evening Star* reported the incident, alleging that the Felixstowe Hospital doctors spoke jocularly of 'Martians' and seemed to consider the explanation given by Geoff and Mavis a tall story. It was suggested they had mistaken the flame from the local propane gas plant flare-stack for a UFO. This the witnesses denied with vehemence.

Bearing in mind the Langenhoe sighting, it seems likely there was something strange in Felixstowe that night. Its nature, however, remains a mystery.

ALIEN VARIATIONS

COULD TODAY'S ALIENS PERHAPS BE THE FAIRIES AND DEMONS OF YESTERYEAR? AND DO SUCH SIGHTINGS MAYBE POINT TO SOME BASIC HUMAN NEED?

On the morning of 4 January 1979, Jean Hingley, a factory worker from near Birmingham in the English Midlands, had what she described as the strangest experience of her whole life. 'At 7 o'clock my husband was going to work by car, and I stood at the back door to wave him off. Hobo, our Alsatian dog, was by my side. When my husband had gone, I saw a light in the garden and thought he had left the light on in the car port. So I went down, but saw that the light was off. As we turned to go back to the house, I saw an orange light over the garden which gradually turned white. It lit the whole garden. We then went into the back door of the house.

'Suddenly, with a sound like *zee . . . zee . . . zee,* three "beings" floated past me through the open door. They glowed with a brilliant light and seemed to float about a foot [30 centimetres] above the floor. As they floated past me into the lounge, I saw that they had wonderful wings.'

Describing the wings in detail, Mrs Hingley said that they glowed with rainbow colours so breathtakingly beautiful that they made our earthly colours look somehow 'chemical'. Both Jean Hingley and her dog were overwhelmed by the experience. The dog flopped on to the floor and lay stiff, as if drugged. Mrs Hingley also felt paralysed. 'After a while the fear seemed to leave me. I felt as if I were lifted up. I seemed to float into the lounge. The three "creatures" were shaking and tugging at the little Christmas tree – three little, slim "men" in silvery-green tunics and silver waistcoats with silver buttons or press studs. They were about 3 feet 6 inches to 4 feet [1 – 1.2 metres] high, all alike. Their pointed hands and feet were covered in the same silvery-green, and they had pointed caps on their heads of the same colour, and with something like a lamp on top. They were floating round the lounge touching everything – the Christmas cards, the clock, the radio and all the furniture. At last, when I could speak, I said: "Three of you and one of me. What are you going to do? What do you want with me?"'

A somewhat awkward conversation followed, in the course of which the creatures revealed that they came from the sky. They said they had visited Australia, New Zealand and America. 'We came down here to try to talk to people, but they don't seem to be interested.'

Although she was very nervous, Jean Hingley talked to them about her life, and they seemed interested in whatever she said. She offered them some mince pies, and when they took them, their hands seemed magnetic. Then she started to show them how to smoke because they seemed curious about her cigarettes, but they were frightened when she lit one, and floated out into the garden.

Jean Hingley herself still seemed to be floating as she followed them. They went towards a glowing, orange-coloured 'space-ship' sitting in her garden. She estimated it to be between 8 and 10 feet (2.4 – 3 metres) long and about 4 feet (1.2 metres) high, with round windows. The creatures still held the mince pies as they entered the object and closed the door. As the craft lifted, they flashed the lights twice – as if, Mrs Hingley thought, saying goodbye. Then the object disappeared. After they had gone, she saw a deep impression in the garden where the 'space-ship' had been; and the packed ice and snow, which had lain for days in the severe winter, had melted away completely.

Many children dream up 'invisible playmates', sometimes resembling fairies, to keep them company – and these 'friends' often become very real. According to one theory, the supernatural creatures seen by adults are more sophisticated 'playmates', called into being for the same kinds of reason that children also need unseen companions.

The entity, left, *was seen by Jean Hingley in 1979, and was one of three who came into her house 'to try to talk to people'.*

Jean Hingley said that, after the beings had left, she felt 'warm and happy . . . as though I had been blessed'.

Many commentators have suggested that today's alien visitors are the space age equivalent of fairies, and a case like Jean Hingley's lends support to such an idea. Both her description and a sketch she made of the aliens could apply just as well to fairies as to extra-terrestrial visitors, and the emphasis on the wings is a particularly noteworthy feature. Although many strange winged creatures have been reported in connection with UFOs – notably by John Keel in his investigation of the 'mothman' sightings in West Virginia in late 1966 – few of the aliens with whom witnesses claim to have made direct contact have had wings.

Historical Parallels

In his classic study *Passport to Magonia,* the ufologist Jacques Vallee presented many examples of similarities between fairy and UFO sightings, and inferred that the two phenomena are basically one. Jean Bastide, in *La Mémoire des Ovni,* took the hypothesis further, saying that 'modern contacts established with extra-terrestrials respect precisely the same rules as contacts in the past with beings more or less human in form.' The parallels are certainly striking, and they have helped to encourage the growth of the notion of 'ancient astronauts'. Adherents claim that many of the anomalous phenomena of the past can best be accounted for by the hypothesis that extra-terrestrials either originated the human race or have interacted with it throughout its history. On the basis of existing evidence, however, this hypothesis remains little more than an intriguing speculation.

On the psychological level, however, there is some reason for supposing that yesterday's fairies were indeed the precursors of today's aliens. Putting aside for a moment the question of the 'reality' of experiences like Jean Hingley's, it is interesting to consider the role played by such entities, their ostensible purpose in manifesting at all, and the effect that their actions have on witnesses.

Right away, we notice that some encounters with entities seem quite accidental and others seem to be clearly directed. Could some manifestations occur in response to a hidden need, a psychological state that calls for outside intervention of some kind? Jean Hingley was certainly in a somewhat troubled state at the time: she had just left her church over a conflict, leaving a gap in her life.

Such considerations have prompted the French ufologist Jean-Francois Boedec, in his book *Fantastiques Rencontres au Bout du Monde,* to suggest that we should conceive of sightings as starting long before the actual experience. Indeed, he points to many cases in which witnesses had premonitions that something was about to happen, or for some reason went home by a different routes or took an unaccustomed walk. Somehow, it would seem, the witnesses were being prepared – or were preparing themselves – for the experience they were about to undergo.

The only way in which this hypothesis could be tested would be by carrying out a psychological examination of every witness, which is hardly possible. We must therefore draw what conclusions we can from what we know of the witnesses' individual circumstances.

It is certainly common for children to dream up 'invisible playmates' to keep them company, and they even sometimes come to believe in the actual existence of these 'friends'. Are fairies, demons and alien visitors perhaps more sophisticated 'playmates', called into being in response to needs, representing our hopes, fears, and expectations?

The illustration, below, *shows a common sort of ufonaut, alongside an elf. The ufologist Jacques Vallee believes that fairy and UFO sightings are two aspects of what is essentially a single phenomenon.*

The sketch,* left, *depicting a spaceship swooping down and capturing three women in Kentucky in 1976, was made by one of the abductees. Many such encounters with UFOs and alien entities seem to have no apparent cause, but others seem to answer a particular need of the witness.

Demons, meanwhile, may meet an intellectual as well as an emotional need. Without demons, theologians would be hard put to account for the existence of evil in the Universe. Consequently, virtually every religion includes not only God, but enemies of God. From this basic assumption, theologians have gone on to picture Earth as the battlefield on which angels and demons fight for people's souls. UFO-related entities have even been identified as agents of Satan.

For an even greater number of people, however, the aliens represent good rather than evil: they are our intellectual and moral superiors who come to Earth to help us sort out our problems – to put an end to wars, social inequality, disease, suffering and all the other evils of the world.

But does it follow that the entities in such cases were conjured up in the witnesses' minds for this purpose?

Some experiences may not be visual at all; or rather, the entity may manifest in a form that seems to rule out altogether any physical identity. Science fiction also contains many variations on the theme of alien invaders 'taking over' humans for sinister purposes. But more people probably still believe that any 'body invaders' are demons from hell rather than aliens from space.

Dr Robert L. Hymers, pastor of the Open Door Community Church in Los Angeles, gives this alarming account of a young man who came to him for help.

'One of our perhaps over-zealous young people had given Don a book to read. The book explained

" ARE THOSE WHO BELIEVE IN THE EXISTENCE OF THESE ENTITIES ALREADY HALFWAY TOWARDS SEEING THEM? "

According to one school of thought, alien sightings – such as that depicted in the artist's impression,* below *– could be projections from the collective unconscious.

"THE HUMAN COLLECTIVE UNCONSCIOUS COULD BE PROJECTING AHEAD OF ITSELF THE IMAGERY WHICH IS NECESSARY FOR OUR OWN LONG-TERM SURVIVAL BEYOND ... THE TWENTIETH CENTURY."

JACQUES VALLEE, REVELATIONS

how people can become demon-possessed through the occult. Don clutched the book and leaned forward in his chair. "I've been reading this book all night, I know I'm demon-possessed. I know it."

"How do you know?" I asked, amid the sounds of his crying.

"I tried to drive over to San Francisco. Something kept grabbing the wheel. Voices in my head kept saying 'Drive off the road! Kill yourself!' I didn't know what to do, so I came here to you... Pastor, please pray for me! Please pray for me now! I'm going insane!"

'I closed my eyes and began. "Father, I pray that you'll give peace to Don. I pray that . . ." but I was stopped by a growling sound, like that of a vicious dog. Dr Hymers then continues:

'I opened my eyes just in time. Don was coming towards me, his fingers moving in a menacing way, his eyes wild, froth dribbling from his mouth. A horrible, vicious voice came from deep in his throat. "I'm going to kill you!"

'I leaped from the chair and dashed to the other side of the room. One thought rushed through my mind. "He's dangerous and he's bigger than me, and I'm alone!" Then I did the only thing I could think of. I pointed my finger at the advancing figure and said, "Demon, I bind thee in the name of Jesus Christ." His body fell heavily to the floor at my feet.

'In the next few minutes, as I bent in prayer over Don's writhing body, he began to grow calm. Finally, he looked up at me. "I feel better now, Pastor," he said.'

Anyone familiar with the current spate of doom-laden tracts from the fundamentalist churches of the United States will recognise that dramatic story as typical of its genre – that of demon possession. The psychiatrist, on the other hand, would be inclined to explain it in terms of an altered state of consciousness in which a suppressed emotion externalises itself, choosing to do so in this dramatic form. Could a similar process be at work in cases where an actual entity is allegedly seen? In the mid-19th century, the French occultist Eliphas Lévi observed: 'He who affirms the devil, creates the devil.' Could this apply to angels and aliens as well? Are those who believe in the existence of these entities already halfway towards seeing them?

Some theologians believe that demons – as represented in a 15th-century French manuscript,* above left *– and angels – depicted on a 19th-century German postcard,* above *– are in a constant battle for people's souls. Such entities may also answer an intellectual need to explain the existence of evil. The idea has even been mooted that fairies and aliens, too, may answer human needs by representing our hopes, fears and expectations.

ENCOUNTERS OF THE FOURTH KIND

ATTEMPTS TO CONTACT INTELLIGENT LIFE ON OTHER PLANETS HAVE SO FAR BEEN UNSUCCESSFUL. BUT WHAT OF THE EVIDENCE FROM PEOPLE WHO CLAIM TO HAVE MET ALIENS?

One wet and windy night in November 1980, Mario Luisi was walking through sodden meadows by a river outside his home village of Burneside in the English Lake District. In the darkness, he saw what he took to be a cow, or even a crudely constructed sheep shelter. But then he saw that the object was hovering 3 feet (1 metre) above the ground and looked far more like a distorted aeroplane. It was about the size of a helicopter and had what seemed to be a tailplane, but no wings. It also bore strange symbols, the like of which Luisi had never seen before.

As he stared at the weird object, glinting in the beam of his lantern, Luisi gradually became aware of a squelching sound and realised that someone was approaching across the soggy ground. Turning the beam in the direction of the sound, he saw two figures, apparently human, about 6 feet (2 metres) away, beside an old oak tree. They were wearing dark, skin-tight suits. At that instant, one of them, apparently female, raised a small, pencil-shaped object in her hand. A bright light shot out from it, striking the face of Luisi's lantern. The glass front shattered and, as Luisi watched, the metal reflector became warped and twisted.

In the scene from Steven Spielberg's film **Close Encounters of the Third Kind**, *below, the protagonist enters a space-ship, surrounded by aliens who seem only able to communicate with human beings with the repetition of a tune of five notes, yet are obviously benevolent. Despite its title, Spielberg's film deals with what UFO experts have now labelled 'close encounters of the fourth kind' – those in which there is intelligent contact with aliens.*

The remainder of Mario Luisi's encounter took place by light emanating from a paper mill on the other side of the river. The female figure spoke to him, telling him that she and her companion meant no harm and that they had come to the Earth in peace. (Presumably, their 'attack' had been a defensive measure against what they had taken to be a weapon – the lantern.) Luisi was told that he must not reveal the strange symbols on the ship, nor those on the lapel badges worn by both figures. He could only stare, his legs shaking, as the two beings, who were fair-skinned, entered their craft by means of a ladder that descended from it. Presently, the object shot upwards, leaving a glow in the sky.

The encounter left Mario Luisi with a memory that was to change his whole outlook on life. For him, at least, there was no longer any doubt – no need to question whether Man is alone in the Universe. He was now certain that we are not.

This question is one that has fascinated mankind ever since it was realised, in the 16th century, that the planets are other worlds, and the stars are other suns, possibly possessing their own planets. Indeed, the human race seems to abhor the idea of being alone in an immeasurably vast Universe. This sentiment was exploited to great effect by Steven Spielberg's epic film *Close Encounters of the Third Kind*, first released in 1977.

Close encounters of the fourth kind, however – of which Mario Luisi's is one – go beyond mere sightings of aliens and involve meeting, talking to, travelling in company with, or even being abducted by creatures not of this world.

Four varieties of close encounters of the fourth kind have been distinguished. Mario Luisi's experience is typical of type *A*, which embraces straightforward encounters where the witness fully remembers what took place. There are no memory blocks, no intervals of time that the subject is unable to recall, and no obvious reasons to doubt that the experience was real.

Such type *A* events provide sober evidence for the reality of aliens. And they are by no means rare. Indeed, over half of all reputed close encounters of the fourth kind are of type *A*.

Although close encounters of the fourth kind as a whole make up no more than about one or two per cent of the total number of UFO reports made each year, this still amounts to many hundreds of cases since the Second World War. They come from almost every country and all social groups: and it is thought that they could be even more common than these figures suggest, for there is evidence that witnesses are frequently unwilling to talk about this kind of experience.

Seeing an unidentified light in the sky is almost commonplace these days, and people are now more willing to report such phenomena than previously. But talking to a creature from another world is, for many people, something to keep quiet about. This is unfortunate, since it means that we cannot be sure of the true scale of the phenomenon. But information supplied by courageous witnesses is sufficient to indicate that something truly extraordinary is going on.

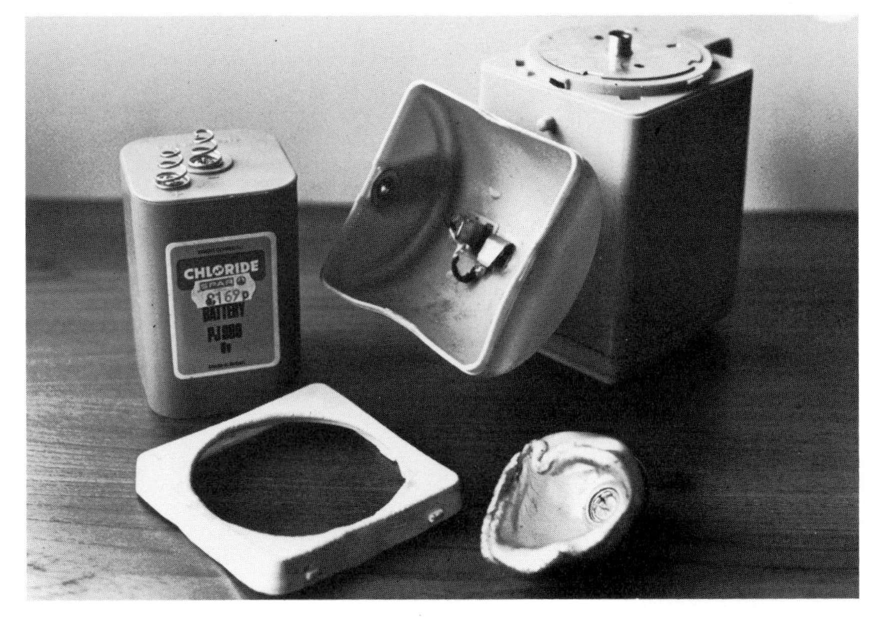

The two aliens, depicted* top, *allegedly visited a Lake District village one stormy November night in 1980. Disturbed by Mario Luisi who was on a night-time stroll, they apparently mistook his lamp for some kind of weapon and destroyed it with a ray gun. Luisi later produced the damaged lamp,* above, *as evidence; but expert analysis established that the damage could have been done with an ordinary blow-torch.

But serious problems arise, even in these seemingly rational type *A* accounts. The Mario Luisi case is typical in this respect. He volunteered the damaged lantern for scientific study, and the results of two independent analyses were found to be identical: in the opinion of experts, the damage had been done by ordinary means, probably by a blow-torch. So had Luisi concocted his story and damaged the lantern himself? If so, it would have been odd for him to be so cooperative. Moreover, it has not been possible to disprove his claim that the lantern was struck by a beam from an alien weapon.

Certain other points in Mario Luisi's story support his statements. But support is not proof: indeed, we never seem to get proof in cases of close encounters of the fourth kind. The difficulty, of course, is that, even if the witness is telling the truth, there is no guarantee that his alien contacts are not using materials and technology indistinguishable from our own. Nevertheless, when what is presented as evidence could perfectly well be of earthly origin, one is bound to become suspicious to a degree.

A number of researchers have conducted studies into close encounters of the fourth kind, analysing the features of the stories in detail. Type *A* cases stand out from other reports in many ways. They tend to occur outside the usual surroundings of the witness, and frequently in the open. They happen at any time of the day, even though UFOs are predominantly nocturnal, and the average number of witnesses per case is well below the average for all UFO cases.

Photographs purporting to show alien beings are, disappointingly, rare. This seems highly significant when it is remembered that UFO photographs are very numerous. If the number of pictures of aliens were in the same proportion as the number of contact cases, then we would have a great deal of material to work on. In fact, there are no more than a few photographs and none that, beyond reasonable doubt, link an alien being with a UFO.

Yet we cannot complacently dismiss the phenomenon as unreal. For there are cases in which several witnesses claim to have seen aliens. One example occurred on 3 March 1980, at Rio Piedras, Puerto Rico. Two teenage children, Vivian and José Rodriguez, were woken at 3.30 a.m. by a barking dog. They looked through the window of their farm to see five strange creatures, with pointed ears and webbed feet, wearing tight-fitting clothes. The aliens seemed interested in the family's chickens. No UFO was observed by the children.

The next day, it was discovered that, at the same time, two men nearby had seen the very same creatures. These witnesses had been sleeping in a parked car, resting during a long journey, and had woken up to see a large domed object that was lying on the ground. Beings who fitted the description given by the two children had emerged

reduce the population. This behaviour, however, seemed to be in conflict with other efforts that they were making to protect us. Our planet, the alien said, was liable to split in half and so they were desperately trying to plug the cracks by injecting a form of liquid cement from their remote-controlled space vehicles.

Interestingly, the witness's wife was in bed beside him all this time, yet she did not wake, nor did it occur to him to disturb her. It seems most unlikely that anyone would make up such a story and expect others to believe it. Indeed, there seems no reason to doubt the witness's sincerity – but neither is it necessary to take this weird story at face value.

Type *B* cases are rarer than type *A*, forming about a quarter of all contact reports, and are almost exclusively single-witness encounters. By far the majority of them occur in the home or its immediate surroundings, and fully two-thirds of the cases occur in the bedroom. Most of them also happen in the early hours of the morning.

Type *A* cases sound like real contacts with something physical; type *B*, on the other hand, sound like some kind of hallucination. This seems a plausible working hypothesis. But there are cases in which it is hard to decide whether a case belongs to type *A* or type *B*.

The third category of contact report, type *C*, involves an occurrence that is not immediately remembered. The experience of an English family, the Days, illustrates how disturbing this can be.

One evening, in October 1974, John and Sue Day were driving to their home at Aveley, in Essex. They had been visiting relatives and were now hurrying, hoping to get back in time to see a late-night

from the object and had then headed in the direction of the Rodriguez farm.

Such a story, if true, is very hard to explain as anything other than a real, physical event, and the apparent subjectivity of these type *A* cases should not be overstressed.

The second group of contact cases, type *B*, is quite different. The aliens involved are often called 'bedroom visitors' because so many of them make their appearance in the bedroom, although witnesses usually claim to have experienced the encounter while wide awake. In fact, these encounters have a good deal in common with ghost sightings that happen in the bedroom.

What distinguishes these events from type *A* cases, however, is that they feature obvious distortions of reality: parts of the sequence of events are completely forgotten, and there are jumps in the story from one scene of action to another, as in a film or a dream.

One such incident took place on 5 January 1980, and concerned a 33-year-old house-painter who awoke at 5 a.m. in his bedroom at Trowbridge, Wiltshire, in southern England. At the foot of his bed, he saw a glowing green figure, 7 feet (2.1 metres) tall, that looked more like a projected image than a solid figure. The alien told the witness that the people to whom he belonged regularly shipped human beings off to other worlds in order to colonise them. When a planet became overcrowded, he was told, they started a war in order to

The illustration,* above, *shows strange creatures with pointed ears and webbed feet, seen examining chickens on a Puerto Rican farm on 3 March 1980. The event falls into the category of close encounter of the fourth kind, 'type A'.

According to the claims of one witness, he was awoken by a tall greenish alien, illustrated* right, *in the early hours of 5 January 1980. The creature said he came from a planet where war is used to control the population level, and that he was trying to prevent the Earth splitting in half by injecting it with cement. This kind of close encounter of the fourth kind, with its obvious conflict with reality, belongs to the category known as 'type B'.

television play. Their three children were with them and had fallen asleep. While on their journey, the parents saw a blue light pacing the car. Intrigued, they watched it for some time, but were unable to identify what it could be.

Then the light disappeared, and the car turned a corner, only to run into a well-defined bank of eerie green mist. The Days were in the mist for only a few seconds, but the car radio sparked and crackled. John instantly yanked out its wires to prevent a fire. After recovering their composure, the family then drove the remaining few hundred yards to their home.

As soon as they arrived, they switched on their television set, but the screen remained blank. It was two hours later than they had thought, and the station had closed down. Someone, or something, had stolen a piece of their lives.

The Days were naturally perturbed by this mysterious time lapse. Over the next few months, they had several dreams about it – fleeting visions of weird faces, and occasional strange impulses to refrain from eating meat or drinking alcohol. Eventually, two UFO investigators, Andy Collins and Barry King, heard of the event and brought in a medical hypnotist – Leonard Wilder. The Days underwent regression hypnosis in the hope of retrieving memories of that missing time. And the memories came.

Under hypnosis, John and Sue gave accounts that were in close agreement. However, there were some differences, and they did indeed claim to have been separated for much of the 'missing' time. The children also seemed to recall the experience in subsequent dreams.

According to the parents' accounts, a UFO had landed and the family had been taken on board. They were given medical examinations, were shown around the craft and informed about its propulsion system, as well as being told about the way of life and intentions of the alien visitors. Eventually, they were returned to their car by a process akin to astral projection, and they continued their journey.

To those who interviewed them, the Day family seemed a group of pleasant and sincere people who had never tried to force their story on to anyone. Something had certainly happened to them that night... but what?

In type *C* contacts, something seems to block the witnesses' memories. Occasionally, however, recall of the 'missing' time is triggered by normal events. Not infrequently, too, the subject has dreams that hint at what took place during the missing minutes, hours – or even, in a very few instances, days. But the most common means by which the floodgates of memory are opened is regression hypnosis.

Type *C* abductions are also remarkably consistent. One in five stories of alien contact involves amnesia and alleged abduction.

Type *C* cases are more subjective than ordinary UFO sightings, too, since they tend to involve fewer witnesses; but they have a higher number of witnesses per case than type *B* or, surprisingly, type *A* cases. The aliens involved usually resemble human beings and are generally of normal human size, or larger: there are very few entities of small stature, unlike those featured in type *A* cases. The most common time for type *C* incidents to occur is between about 10 p.m. and midnight; and a very large proportion of them involve young couples driving cars along quiet roads (quite often carrying children with them). It is also common for one or more of the witnesses to have a history of strange experiences – seeing ghosts or poltergeist activity, for example.

The fourth group of close encounters of the fourth kind – type *D* – comprises very few cases, and consists of experiences in which the encounter does not seem to involve physical contact. Rather, communication occurs by means of what seems to be telepathy or automatic writing. Whatever the category of the close encounter, however, it is obvious that many people sincerely believe they have been contacted by alien beings, and this alone is surely enough to warrant continued serious investigation of the phenomenon.

Perhaps the strangest category of close encounter of the fourth kind is that known as 'type C' – in which witnesses are subject to loss of memory following their experience. The Day family of Aveley, Essex, England, underwent this after the events of one October night in 1974. They were driving home when, they claimed, they encountered a UFO that interfered with their car radio; and when they arrived back home, they found it was two hours later than they thought. It subsequently emerged under hypnosis that they believed they had been taken aboard a UFO by aliens, illustrated below, and subjected to medical examinations.

> " IF IT WERE NOT FOR THE FACT THAT I HAVE SPOKEN WITH A NUMBER OF COMPLETELY HONEST CLOSET CONTACTEES AROUND THE WORLD, WHO CLAIM TO HAVE HAD SIMILAR EXPERIENCES, I WOULD HAVE REJECTED SUCH STORIES LONG AGO. "
>
> **TIMOTHY GOOD, ALIEN LIAISON**

CASEBOOK

GREEN-FINGERED ALIENS

VISITING HUMANOIDS ARE REPORTED TO HAVE TAKEN A KEEN INTEREST IN CULTIVATED PLANTS DURING SEPARATE INCIDENTS IN FRANCE AND IN SPAIN. WHAT COULD HAVE BEEN THEIR PURPOSE?

Ufologists often lament the fact that so few UFO sightings are made by people with 'trained minds' – by which they mean scientists and engineers. But this is not really surprising, since the 'trained mind' of a witness is likely to harbour prejudices that discourage him from reporting an extraordinary experience and, instead, encourage him to explain it away. On the other hand, unsophisticated observers, unacquainted with the UFO controversy, are often impressive witnesses, telling their stories without embroidering them. Indeed, the classic sightings of 'flying saucers' described here may have more value by virtue of coming from people of little formal education or technical training.

In the artist's impression, **below,** *an oval UFO stands in a lavender field in south-east France, while two aliens examine plants that are growing close to their craft.*

Just after 5 a.m. on 1 July 1965, Maurice Masse, a 41-year-old lavender grower, set to work in his fields situated on the Valensole plateau in the Basses Alpes of south-eastern France. At about 5.45 a.m., he stopped to have a cigarette, parking his tractor by a hillock at the end of a small vineyard that lay along the northern side of the field.

Suddenly, he heard a shrill whistling noise and glanced round the hillock, fully expecting to see a helicopter: instead, he saw a dull-coloured object the size of a Renault Dauphine car, and shaped like a rugby football, with a cupola on top. It was standing on six metallic legs, and there was also a central support, which appeared to be stuck into the ground. Close to the 'machine', Masse saw two boys, about eight years old, bending over a lavender plant.

Masse crossed the vineyard and approached the boys, believing them to be the vandals who had picked young shoots from a number of his lavender plants on several occasions during the preceding month. Then, to his surprise, he saw that he was not approaching boys at all, but two dwarf-like creatures with large bald heads. He was about 15 feet (5 metres) from the beings when one of them turned and pointed a pencil-like instrument at him.

Maurice Masse,* below, *owner of vast lavender fields in south-eastern France, stands on the area where a UFO stood while he watched, unable to move. Only weeds would grow in this patch of land after the incident.

One of the aliens,* bottom, *is depicted pointing some sort of weapon – perhaps an immobiliser – at the French farmer.

Immediately he was stopped in his tracks, unable to move any part of his body. (In the first reports of the case, it was stated that the witness was 'paralysed', but UFO investigator Aimé Michel suggested the term 'immobilised', perhaps by some form of hypnotic suggestion.)

According to Masse's description, the creatures were less than 4 feet (1.2 metres) tall, and were wearing close-fitting grey-green overalls. They had huge pumpkin-shaped heads, but no hair – only smooth white skin. Their cheeks were wide and fleshy, narrowing to very pointed chins; the eyes were large and slanting. The witness did not mention their noses, but he did describe the mouths, which were like thin slits and opened to form lipless holes. (It is rare in close encounters for humanoids to be reported as having their heads uncovered outside the craft, as in this case.)

Body-Talk

The creatures appeared to communicate with each other, but not with their mouths, for inarticulate sounds seemed to come from the mid-body region. The hapless lavender grower thought they were mocking him, although he admitted that their glances were not hostile; indeed, he never had the impression he was face-to-face with monsters. Masse has never disclosed what took place during the rest of the time he was immobilised, 15 feet (5 metres) from the beings.

After a few minutes, the creatures returned to their machine, moving in a remarkable manner, 'falling and rising in space like bubbles in a bottle without apparent support . . . sliding along bands of light . . .', to enter the object through a sliding door. The witness said he could see them looking at him from inside the craft. Suddenly, there was a thump from the central support, which retracted, the six legs began to whirl, and the machine floated away at an angle of 45°, making a shrill whistling sound. At 65 feet (20 metres), it just disappeared, although traces of its passage in the direction of Manosque were found on lavender plants for more than 100 yards (90 metres). (Mysteriously, these plants withered, then later recovered and grew taller and finer than those nearby.)

The farmer grew alarmed as the invisible bonds that held him failed to relax their grip, but after 15 minutes he slowly regained use of his limbs. He could see marks left by some of the legs of the craft, and almost liquid mud around the hole where the central support had entered the ground. (This was odd, since there had been no rain in the area for several weeks.)

Masse ran down to Valensole, on the outskirts of which is the *Café des Sports.* The proprietor, a friend, was just opening for the day, and Masse, shaken and as white as a sheet, told him part of his story. The café owner pressed Masse for further details of what had happened, but the farmer refused to say any more because he feared the rest of his story would not be believed. His friend advised him to report the incident to the police, but Masse would not. So the café proprietor rushed to the field, saw the marks and returned to tell Masse's story for himself.

That evening, Masse took his 18-year-old daughter to see the landing site: now they saw that only four of the craft's legs had left marks on the ground, and that the mud around the central hole had set like concrete.

The World's Reaction

Soon after Masse's experience was made public, he was questioned by the chief of the local police. Crowds of sightseers visited the field, and Valensole was flooded with representatives of the press, radio and television. On 4 July, overwhelmed with interviews and questions, Masse collapsed, seized with an insuperable desire to sleep. It was reported that he would have slept for 24 hours a day had his wife not awakened him to make him eat.

The initial private investigation was conducted by a local magistrate, who handed his report to *Flying Saucer Review* in October 1965. He said that Masse had prevented his daughter approaching too close to the hole for he feared she might suffer some harmful effect from it: indeed, he was also worried about any possible genetic effects it might have on himself. In the end, he filled the hole, which was shaped like an inverted funnel.

Aimé Michel interviewed the witness twice at Valensole in 1965, and found him anxious and distressed, still worried about possible effects on his health. During his second visit, Michel showed Masse a photograph of a model based on a description of a UFO seen at Socorro, New Mexico, in 1964. Masse was staggered that someone should have photographed his machine; but when told that it was actually a picture of a craft that had been seen in the USA by a policeman, he sighed with relief: 'You see, then, that I wasn't dreaming, and that I'm not mad'.

Two years later, UFO investigators visited Maurice Masse again and he took them to see the landing site. It was 10 feet (3 metres) in diameter, and still distinguishable because lavender plants around the perimeter were withered, and only weeds grew in the inner area, despite the fact that it had been ploughed and replanted since the time of the original incident.

Although Masse had recovered from his experience, he was anxious to avoid any more publicity. So, in an endeavour to hide the location of the landing site, he trimmed the mass of weeds to the shape of lavender plants. Eventually, he tore up the vineyard, ploughed the lavender field and then sowed it all with wheat.

The Alfalfa Factor

In 1974, *Flying Saucer Review* received a report from the Charles Fort Group of Valladolid in Spain, who had investigated a UFO sighting that had been made some years earlier. The witness was a 22-year-old woman, a domestic employee in the house of a farmer at Puente de Herrera, close by the river Duero, south of Valladolid. The young woman's name was withheld, at her request, as she had received no primary education, and was illiterate.

On the night of 15 August 1970, the señorita had been watching television when she heard a piercing whistling noise. At the same time, the television picture was suddenly blotted out by a mass of lines. Playing with the controls had no effect, so she switched off the set and then went to the front door of the house to investigate the noise.

There, she was astounded to see a weird object with various lights standing on the drive. Nearby stood a strange-looking 'man' who seemed to be surveying a crop of alfalfa in an adjacent field. Very scared, the young woman went back inside the house and shut the door. Then the whistling sound began again; but, when she went to look out of the window, both machine and 'man' had gone.

***During a close encounter in northern Spain, an alien surveyed an alfalfa field while his craft flashed coloured lights, as shown in the illustration* below.**

The señorita told only her boyfriend of her experience at the time. Members of her family became aware of it only in March 1972 when, after her brother-in-law had made some observation about UFOs, she told them about what she had seen. It was her brother-in-law who passed the information to the Charles Fort Group.

During the investigation that followed, J. Macias and his fellow researchers learned that the period of time between the onset of the whistling noise and the witness first looking out of the window was about 5 minutes. The whistling noise persisted while she was peering through the door, but seemed a little less intense. She had switched off the porch lights as she usually did between 10.30 and 11.00 p.m., so she felt nobody could have seen her when she opened the door.

The UFO, which was balanced on several 'feet' on the road surface, was about 12 feet (4 metres) wide and 8 feet (2.5 metres) high. The upper part consisted of a hemispherical cupola, which seemed to be made of crystal. On top of this, a bluish-white light revolved erratically, the light dimming whenever it slowed down. The cupola was supported by a disc surrounded with a ring of coloured lights that constantly changed from white to purple and then again to yellow.

The occupant of the craft was about 5 feet 10 inches (1.8 metres) tall and was dressed in a dark, tight-fitting garment and a helmet. Around his ankles and wrists there were glowing white 'bracelets', and in the middle of his belt was a square 'buckle' of similar iridescent material. The señorita was not sure about the colour of his skin, and could not see any hair. She said the 'man' seemed to be interested in the alfalfa, and walked towards it with unusually long strides.

A Persistent Afterglow

According to the witness, physical vestiges of the craft were left at the landing site for, when she went to the window of her room, she saw a soft glow where the object had been standing. Intrigued by this, she inspected the ground. On the surface of the road there were black footprints, similar to those made by ordinary shoes, the heel mark narrower than that of the sole. The marks must have been seen by everybody coming to the house, but the señorita told no one of her experience at the time and therefore did not draw attention to them. While they remained, however, the area where the UFO had landed continued to glow at night.

The investigators considered that the señorita's illiteracy added to the authenticity of her account on the grounds that she could hardly have fabricated a story of such complexity. After speaking with members of her family, they realised that their knowledge of other UFO encounters was insufficient for her to have picked up such detailed data from them either. Furthermore, there seemed to be no motivation for a hoax, for it was only by chance that she mentioned her experience to her brother-in-law 18 months after the event. Other members of the family later told the investigators that, after their first interview with the señorita, she had wept hysterically and rounded on her brother-in-law for having given away her secret.

THE ALIENS STRIKE BACK

EXTRA-TERRESTRIALS DO NOT ALWAYS BEHAVE PEACEABLY, IT SEEMS. INDEED, THE ACCOUNTS GIVEN HERE INVOLVE ALIENS WHO SHOWED REMARKABLY VIOLENT TENDENCIES

It has been claimed that UFO experiences are conjured up in the minds of the beholders – in other words, that the objects and any occupants are actually created by the percipients. If there is any truth in this, then powerful minds must indeed have been at work in the incidents cited below. Witnesses were manhandled, scratched and almost carried off by UFO occupants. However, in all these cases, more than one person was present, so there is unlikely to have been a question of mere hallucination. Some external stimulus must have been involved – such as an extra-terrestrial or meta-terrestrial entity, encountered either directly or through some form of projection, or perhaps by means of remote control of the witnesses' perceptions and mental processes.

The first case occurred at 2 a.m. on 28 November 1954, when two young men – travelling in a van near Caracas, Venezuela – came upon a luminous sphere, about 10 feet (3 metres) wide, hovering 6 feet (2 metres) above the road. One of the men, Gustavo González, got out to investigate; but as he approached the UFO, he was set upon by a slight, dwarf-like, bristly creature, who sent him sprawling with a casual push. The humanoid then leapt on González, its eyes glowing. González drew a knife and lashed out at his adversary, but the blade glanced off the creature's hairy body as if from a rock.

Then another creature appeared and momentarily dazzled González with a powerful light. González's companion, José Ponce, jumped from the van and came to help his friend. Next, he saw two more creatures emerge from the roadside bushes, carrying rocks. All four then leapt effortlessly into the hovering craft and were gone.

The two men reported the incident to the police. A doctor who examined them had been out on an emergency call and had seen the fracas from a distance. Both men were found to be suffering from shock and fright, and González had a long, deep scratch on his side.

Less than two weeks after this encounter, on 10 December 1954, Lorenzo Flores and Jesús Gomez were on a hunting expedition near Carora, Venezuela, when they saw a luminous object about 10 feet (3 metres) across and shaped like two wash basins placed one on top of the other. It was hovering just above ground level, and flames were coming out of its underside.

In the illustration, **below**, *a dwarf-like, bristly alien is about to attack Gustavo González on a road near Caracas, Venezuela, in 1954. In the background is the luminous sphere of the spaceship.*

PHYSICAL ATTACK

The youths said that four small, dark and hirsute creatures, with rock-like bodies, climbed out of the craft and attacked them. When they began to drag Gomez away, Flores struck one with the butt of his unloaded shotgun, but the weapon broke in two. They managed to escape from their assailants and reach a police station, but both boys were covered in deep scratches, and were extensively bruised, while their clothes were badly torn.

Six days later, on 16 December, in the Venezuelan town of San Carlos del Zulia, Jesús Paz was a passenger in a car with some friends, and asked the driver to pull over so he could relieve himself in some bushes. His companions were waiting for him to return when they heard a loud scream. They rushed into the bushes and found Paz lying unconscious, while a small humanoid was seen scurrying towards a shiny, hovering, disc-like object. It climbed aboard and the craft soared away, making a whistling sound as it went. When examined later, Paz was found to be covered in deep scratches on his right side and down his spine.

Yet another of these bizarre stories of violent behaviour by strange UFO entities was reported from Sweden in 1958. Hans Gustavsson, aged 25, and his friend, 30-year-old Stig Rydberg, had been to a dance on the evening of 20 December. Returning home to Halsingborg, they had reached a place called Domsten, when they saw a saucer-shaped object with three 'legs' resting on the ground. It seemed to measure about 16 feet (5 metres) across and 3-feet (1 metre) high, and was illuminated from within by a light that was neither fierce nor warm. It had what appeared to be a dark core at its centre.

During an encounter in Sweden in 1958, two friends returning from a late-night dance were attacked by the four limbless aliens, depicted* above. *Their space-craft gave off a light, at the centre of which was a dark core.

"THEY SEEMED TO HAVE NO LIMBS, YET SOMEHOW APPEARED TO MAKE A GRAB FOR THE MEN, TRYING TO DRAG THEM TOWARDS THE CRAFT... RYDBERG STRUCK AT AN ASSAILANT, BUT HIS ARM MERELY SANK INTO THE CREATURE, RIGHT UP TO THE ELBOW."

The UFO illustrated* below *was seen by several witnesses on a farm near Anolaima, Colombia. The encounter may have led to the death of one of them.

The two men looked at the spectacle for a few minutes, and then came under attack. Four grey creatures, each about 3 feet (1 metre) tall, rushed towards them. They seemed to have no limbs, yet somehow appeared to make a grab for the men, trying to drag them towards the craft. Gustavsson and Rydberg struggled but found it almost impossible to get a hold on the jelly-like creatures. Rydberg struck at an assailant, but his arm merely sank into the creature, right up to the elbow.

The attackers suddenly decided to concentrate on Gustavsson, whereupon Rydberg ran to the car and sounded the horn to attract attention. At the sudden blast of noise, the creatures ran off, boarded their craft, and flew away.

TRAGIC DEATH

In July 1969, representatives of the Aerial Phenomena Research Organisation (APRO) received information about another startling UFO incident that had taken place on a farm near Anolaima, some 40 miles (65 kilometres) from Bogotá, Colombia. A particularly careful investigation of the case was made as one of the witnesses, Arcesio Bermudez, died just eight days after this particular sighting.

On the evening of 4 July, Bermudez and some of his family and friends – five adults and four children in all – were talking inside the farmhouse when they heard shouts from 13-year-old Mauricio Gnecco, who was outside with another child, Enrique Osorio. The group went outside and saw a yellow-orange light moving across the sky about 600 feet (180 metres) away. Mauricio began signalling to the object with a flashlight, whereupon it immediately increased its speed and approached the house. It stopped about 50 yards (45 metres) away and hovered between two tall trees for about five seconds, but made no sound whatsoever. The witnesses estimated the height of the object as between 4 and 6 feet (1.2 – 1.8 metres) and said that it seemed to have an 'arc of light' surrounding it, and two blue luminous legs with green tips.

When the object again began to move, Arcesio Bermudez ran towards it, taking with him Mauricio's flashlight. Mauricio and one of the other children watched from a nearby hill and reported that the object 'blinked on and off', then rose in the sky and moved off in the direction of Bogotá.

Bermudez returned to the farmhouse and described what he had seen to the others. He said that he had been within 20 feet (6 metres) of the object, that it had 'blinked off' and that he had seen a 'person' inside. From the waist down, the entity seemed to be shaped like a letter *A* and was luminous, but otherwise Bermudez thought it was 'normal'. The object then 'blinked on', rose into the sky and simply disappeared. A few minutes later, the object – or another identical one – was seen travelling slowly across the sky at a height of about 300 feet (90 metres). At approximately the same time, two other people – Clemente Bolivar and Rosalba Prieto, who lived 2 miles (3 kilometres) from the farmhouse – also saw a bright orange-yellow light moving slowly towards Bogotá.

Two days after the sighting, Arcesio Bermudez was taken ill. According to the APRO researchers' report: 'His temperature dropped to 95°F [35°C], and he had a "cold touch", although he claimed he did not feel cold. Within a few days, his condition became far more serious; he had "black vomit" and diarrhoea with blood flow.' Bermudez was taken to Bogotá where, on 12 July, he was attended first by Dr Luis Borda and later by Dr Cesar Esmeral, neither of whom knew of his UFO sighting. Just before midnight, Arcesio Bermudez died, the cause of death diagnosed as gastroenteritis.

Four days later, John Simhon of APRO interviewed the surviving witnesses and invited the children to draw what they had seen. At 8 p.m. on the same day, four of the children were placed in hypnotic trance by Dr Luis E. Martinez of the National University of Colombia to see if any more details of their experience would be revealed. Their accounts tallied almost exactly with earlier statements and also with those given by adult witnesses. While under hypnosis, the children also drew pictures of the 'flying saucer' and these were found to be much the same as their earlier drawings.

On 17 July, Simhon and Elias Nessim (also of APRO) accompanied the witnesses to the scene of the sighting, but no physical evidence of the UFO was found. Further questioning revealed that only Bermudez had claimed to have seen the object land. One of the other witnesses, Luis Carbajal, said that he had heard Bermudez calling him to go to look at the object, but stated that he had only seen it flying away between the trees. The investigators pointed out that the farmhouse lies on an air route to Bogotá International Airport and suggested that the object could have been a conventional aircraft. However, all the witnesses stated that what they had seen was definitely not an aeroplane.

Simhon then sent details of Bermudez's illness, together with his clothes and wrist watch, to the Colombian Institute of Nuclear Affairs, and was informed – unofficially – that Bermudez's symptoms seemed similar to those caused by gamma rays.

Other specialists were also provided with details of the Bermudez case. Dr Horace C. Dudley, professor of radiation physics at the University of Illinois Medical Center in Chicago, stated: 'The illness and death of Mr Bermudez may be due to radiation

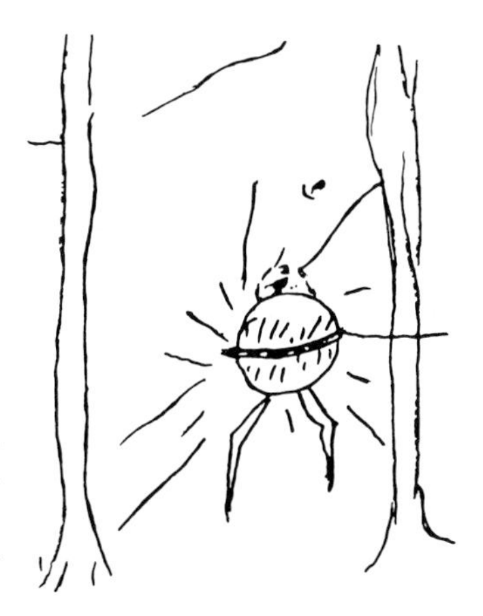

These drawings of the Anolaima UFO were made, top, by Mauricio Gnecco, aged 13, while in hypnotic trance and, above, by Enrique Osorio, aged 12, in a normal waking state.

The UFO seen on a farm in Fort Beaufort, South Africa – and pictured in the artist's impression, below – frequently changed colour, from red to green and yellow. On its top was what seemed to be a bright star.

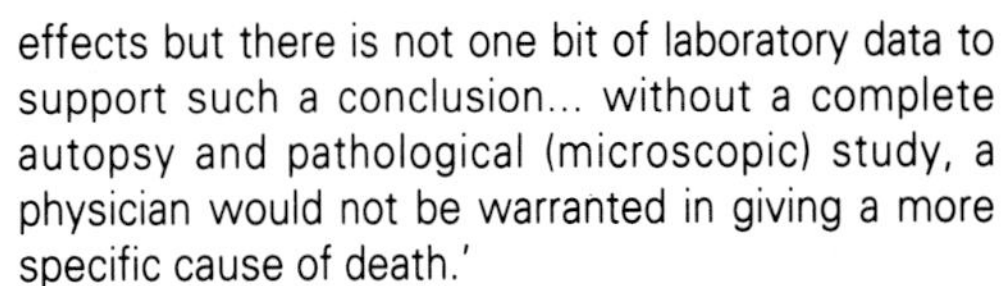

effects but there is not one bit of laboratory data to support such a conclusion... without a complete autopsy and pathological (microscopic) study, a physician would not be warranted in giving a more specific cause of death.'

APRO consultant in medicine Dr Benjamin Sawyer reported: 'The symptoms of enteritis . . . are nearly identical to one of the three basic forms of [intestinal] illness from radiation exposure. There is nothing superficially apparent to distinguish the two illnesses.' But there was insufficient evidence to determine whether death was due to enteritis or radiation poisoning.

Sometimes, however, it is assumed that aliens must be hostile, as a case from South Africa clearly shows. Here, a farmer, Bernardus Smit, fired shots at a UFO seen on his farm. The incident happened on 26 June 1972 on Smit's property, in the eastern Cape Province. It was a bright and sunny winter's morning. Smit was working in a field when one of his labourers came running towards him. The man had gone to inspect an irrigation dam, when he saw smoke coming from a clump of trees. As he approached, he saw a shiny object with a bright star on top emerge from the trees and hover overhead. The labourer raced back to warn Smit, who decided to go and see for himself.

Smit saw the UFO in thick scrub, where it was glowing bright red. It then changed to green and yellow. He hurried home, telephoned the police, returned at once to the site with his .303 rifle and fired at the object.

Two policemen arrived at 10 a.m. More shots were fired from a distance of about 275 yards (250 metres). By this time, the UFO was a grey colour. When Smit hit the star on the top of it, the UFO ceased changing colour, but it emitted a humming sound and disappeared into impenetrable bush. One of the policemen later said that the UFO was of a darkish hue but shone in the centre and had a surrounding glow. Marks were later found cut into the ground where the object had been.

Subsequently, a newspaper commentator made this observation:

'I suppose the good men at Fort Beaufort were only behaving in the traditional South African way of life – what we don't understand, we shoot.'

As it happened, the Fort Beaufort incident proved to be the forerunner of a wave of UFO sightings in South Africa.

> " WHATEVER UFOs ARE, THEY ARE REAL AND SHOULD NOT BE TAKEN LIGHTLY... UFOs MAY OR MAY NOT BE SIGNIFICANT TO MANKIND IN THE LONG RUN; BUT UNTIL WE FIND OUT, WE SHOULD TREAT THEM WITH THE GREATEST OF CAUTION. "
>
> **BOB PRATT, UFO RESEARCHER**

CASEBOOK

A GIANT, FACELESS HUMANOID, THE STRANGE TELEPORTATION OF CATTLE, AND A CAR-CHASING UFO – JUST SOME OF THE MANY PHENOMENA ALLEGEDLY EXPERIENCED BY THE COOMBS FAMILY AT RIPPERSTON FARM, WALES

UNRAVELLING THE RIPPERSTON RIDDLE

During the autumn of 1977, an enterprising hotelier in west Wales began to offer special weekend breaks for UFO investigators. Enthusiasts would be free to use the hotel facilities all night long, and an expert would guide them to the most favourable locations for UFO spotting, though sighting was, of course, not guaranteed. 'Pembrokeshire is quite a way ahead in this sort of thing,' the hotelier observed at the time; and she professed herself flabbergasted at the number of people who had written or telephoned in order to make enquiries.

What was drawing the attention of UFO enthusiasts, not only from Britain but also from abroad, was the continuous flow of remarkable reports from what the press now called 'the Broad Haven triangle'. Serious ufologists have learned to be cautious about 'flaps'. Periods when more than the usual number of reports come in may genuinely represent an increased level of activity, but it may simply be that the publication of reports encourages witnesses to come forward when otherwise they would have kept their experiences quiet. No more incidents may have occurred: it is just that more are disclosed. There is, of course, the further possibility that news about sightings may stimulate some people to have imaginary experiences.

Such possibilities are anathema, however, to those ufologists who are convinced that all UFO sightings are grounded in physical fact and who deny that there may be a psychological aspect to such experiences. But the possibility that some kind of 'contagion of ideas' was operating in west Wales during the spring and summer of 1977 is certainly suggested by many of the reports – most of all by the series of astonishing events that were alleged to have taken place at Ripperston Farm, and that focus on the Coombs family. So completely did these events capture the public imagination that

Ripperston Farm, near St Brides Bay in west Wales,* left, *was the home of the Coombs family who reported many seemingly paranormal events in the spring and summer of 1977. One of the striking aspects of this case is that Brian and Caroline Klass, whose cottage adjoined that of the Coombs, did not see or hear anything unusual at this time – or at least chose not to publicise any experiences.

three books were wholly or in large part devoted to them. There was too, extensive coverage by press and television. Unfortunately, this resulted in so much contradiction and confusion that the true facts have been difficult to establish. In what follows, the most probable version of the truth has been selected; but frequently it has been a matter of choosing between contradictory accounts, and absolute accuracy cannot be guaranteed.

Billie Coombs was a herdsman, one of three men responsible for looking after the dairy herd at Ripperston Farm on behalf the farm manager, Richard Hewison, who lived at neighbouring Lower Broadmoor Farm and who was in turn responsible to the company that owned both farms. Billie and his wife Pauline lived with their five children in a cottage on Ripperston Farm. Immediately next door was another cottage, where Brian Klass, also a Ripperston employee, lived with his wife Caroline.

Although Pauline Coombs had reported some earlier UFO experiences, the first major event occurred on 16 April. She was driving home one evening after dark, together with three of her children, when her 10-year-old son Keiron, who was in the back seat, reported a strange light in the sky. It was about the shape and size of a rugby ball, luminous, yellowish, with a hazy, greyish light underneath and had a torch-like beam shining down from it. Keiron told his mother that the light had U-turned and was following them. The object caught up with the car and travelled along beside it, at which point the car lights started to fade. Near the house, the engine cut out altogether, so that Pauline had to coast the rest of the way. She ran in to call her husband. He and their eldest son, Clinton, came out just in time to see the UFO heading out to sea. When Billie tried to start the car, he found that it now functioned perfectly.

Pauline Coombs was driving along the road leading to Ripperston Farm,* above, *when – she claimed – the car was chased by a UFO, shown in the artist's impression,* left. *She and the children were terrified; and their fear increased when, as they approached the house, the car engine and lights cut out completely so that they had to coast the rest of the way home.

A few weeks later, Pauline reported seeing another UFO from her kitchen window. It was apparently about 20 feet (6 metres) in diameter and rested about 3 feet (1 metre) off the ground. Silvery in colour, it had antennae and a tripod undercarriage. It again took off towards the sea, leaving a circular 'burn mark'. On another occasion, two of the younger children claimed to have seen three UFOs in the sky, circular in shape and with domes. One was only about 50 feet (15 metres) above the ground, and from it a ladder was lowered, down which the children saw a silver-suited figure climb. The UFO also dropped a bright red, fluorescent box-like object into the grass of the field: later, the children looked for the box but it had disappeared.

On 22 April, Mr and Mrs Coombs were watching a late-night film on television, despite interference, which was particularly bad that evening. At about 11.30 p.m., Pauline became aware of a glow outside the uncurtained sitting-room window. An hour or so later, her husband saw a face at the window. 'It was a man – but a terrible size,' he later reported, estimating the height of the figure at nearly 7 feet (2 metres). The creature was wearing a white suit. Its face – if it had one – was concealed behind a kind of black visor.

Terrified, Coombs telephoned first the farm manager, Richard Hewison, and then Randall Jones Pugh, the local British UFO Research Association investigator. Pugh advised him to inform the police. Hewison came round at once, followed by the police, but they found no trace of the intruder. About three weeks later, a similar figure was sighted by the eight-year-old twins. They were out in the fields, 'playing roly-poly in the grass', when they saw an entity that they described in almost the same terms as their parents: again, it was dressed in silver, with a black head. It walked past them, about 50 feet (15 metres) away, and then it disappeared, apparently having walked straight through a barbed-wire fence.

A Strange Disappearance

But of all the events that were reported from Ripperston Farm, certainly the most bizarre was the seemingly supernatural movement of cattle. On several occasions, Billie Coombs found that the cattle in his care – sometimes only one or two animals, but frequently the entire herd – had disappeared from the yard. On at least one occasion, he subsequently received an angry telephone call from a neighbouring farmer, asking him to come to collect his herd. Billie insisted that the animals had been properly fastened in, adding that he had even secured the bolt with binder twine as an extra precaution. To escape in the way indicated, the herd would have had to move directly past the cottage: yet neither Billie nor his wife had heard a sound. On one occasion, he reported, there simply had not been enough time between the moment at which the cattle had last been seen and the moment when they were reported to be at another farm for them to have traversed the distance in any natural way. The implication seemed to be that they had somehow been spirited from one place to the other. The cattle definitely appeared badly frightened, and next day the milk yield was down.

This extraordinary movement of cattle presents the toughest challenge to credulity. The UFO and entity sightings, remarkable as they are, fall within a commonly accepted range of phenomena; but teleportation of animals seems to belong to a completely different class.

This last case seems to point to poltergeist activity, which raises the question of whether a similar agency was at work at Ripperston. If so, it was a particularly powerful one: the teleportation of an entire herd of cattle definitely transcends any poltergeist phenomenon ever reported. Nonetheless, other events reported from Ripperston might be seen as supporting the poltergeist hypothesis. It is noteworthy, for example, that the place seemed to exert a highly malevolent influence on mechanical objects. Apart from the alarming failure of Pauline Coombs' car right at the climax of her frightening UFO chase, Billie Coombs reported that he had found it necessary to replace his car five times during 1977 alone and that they suffered an even higher accident rate with television sets. Again, the family's electricity bill was so extraordinarily high that they were forced to ask the Electricity Board to inspect the meters. Oddly, no fault was found.

The suggestion that psychic forces may have been at work is supported by details concerning the earlier history of Pauline Coombs, who was by faith a Roman Catholic. Some time before coming to Ripperston, the Coombs family had been living in a caravan at nearby Pembroke Dock. Here, strange

It is not, however, entirely without precedent. In his book *Haunted Houses,* John Ingrams describes a strange report from Birchen Bower, near Oldham in Lancashire. At this house, a macabre custom was observed. A former owner, terrified of being buried alive, had refused to allow her body to be buried. Instead, she left instructions that it should be embalmed and brought to the house every 21 years, where it was to be left in a granary for a week. This had a weird effect on the livestock:

'In the morning, when the corpse was fetched, the horses and cows were always found let loose, and sometimes a cow would be found up in the hay-loft, although how it came there was, indeed, a mystery, as there was no passage large enough to admit a beast of such magnitude... A few years ago, when a cow belonging to the farmer then tenanting the place was found in the hay-loft, it was the firm belief of many thereabouts that supernatural agency had been employed to place it there... How the cow was got up was a mystery to everyone, whilst that blocks had to be borrowed from Bower Mill to let it down through the hay-hole outside the barn was an equally well-known fact.'

The *Daily Mail* of 18 May 1906 also noted, in the course of a report on a disturbed house: 'A horse vanished from the barn and was found in the hay room. A partition had to be knocked down to get him out.' And in April 1936, the Italian journal *Ali del Pensiero* reported:

'Phenomena of incendiary infestation have been recently established on a farm in Prignano (Salerno); fires broke out spontaneously, destroyed household objects, and burned persons and animals. Bricks and stones fell in the rooms, although the windows were closed. There was spontaneous displacement of objects. A pair of oxen... were carried from one stall to another without human agency... A doctor and psychical researcher found a 16-year-old girl with strong mediumistic faculties who was the involuntary means of the striking phenomena.'

***From her kitchen window, Pauline Coombs saw a UFO flying towards the sea, as depicted* above.**

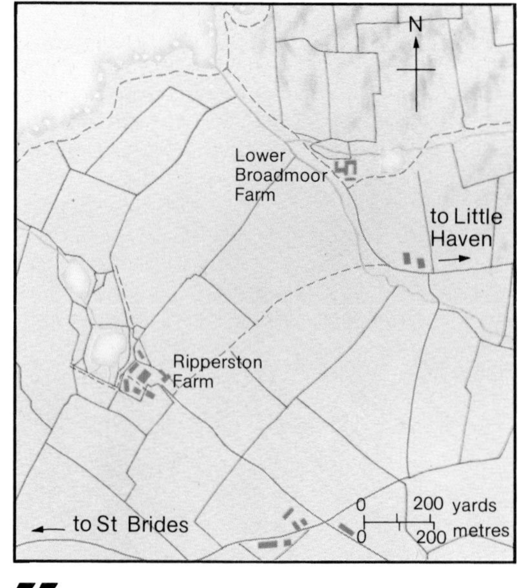

The map,* right, *shows the position of Ripperston Farm in relation to that of Lower Broadmoor Farm. On several occasions, Billie Coombs reported that cattle had mysteriously disappeared from his yard – even though he had secured the gate – only to turn up at Broadmoor Farm, a half-mile (800 metres) away. Local BUFORA investigator Randall Jones Pugh,* below, *visited the farm but could find no explanation for the mystery.

" THE PROLIFERATION OF INCIDENTS AT RIPPERSTON FARM MADE IT A FOCUS OF INTEREST FOR REPORTERS AND INVESTIGATORS ALIKE... SO PERHAPS IT WAS ONLY TO BE EXPECTED THAT SOONER OR LATER FIGURES, VERY MUCH LIKE THE SINISTER MEN IN BLACK, SHOULD BE REPORTED AS TURNING UP. "

manifestations also began to occur. Every evening, from the inside of the caravan, Pauline would see a life-size apparition of the Virgin, wearing a white dress. She had a rosary tied round her waist and was holding the child Jesus. Later, the figure became that of Jesus on his own, and would remain for some half-an-hour. Word got around, and soon every evening a crowd of sightseers would turn up, hoping to catch sight of the phenomenon. Eventually, the owner of the caravan had it destroyed because he was annoyed by this constant flow of visitors. As reported, this incident is very unsatisfactory. Caravan owners do not usually resort to destroying their own property, even for such a reason. However, for our purpose, the suggestion is clear that there was already some quality about Pauline Coombs that might make her prone to strange experiences.

Pauline Coombs is seen* above, *at the window through which she and her husband saw a humanoid at about 1 a.m. on 23 April 1977. She had noticed a 'glow' at the window an hour or so beforehand, but decided not to mention it to her husband because she believed he would think she was 'suffering from nerves'. Then he saw a creature, a silver-suited man of 'a terrible size', pressed right up against the window, as in the illustration,* right. *The police were called, but they found no signs of an intruder.

SINISTER VISITORS

The proliferation of incidents at Ripperston Farm made it a focus of interest for reporters and investigators alike, on and off throughout the spring and summer of 1977: so perhaps it was only to be expected that sooner or later figures, very much like the sinister men in black who so often visit witnesses to UFO landings, should be reported as turning up at the farm. One day, so the account alleges, an unusual car suddenly drove up, but silently, so that no one heard it approach. It contained two men who were remarkably similar to one another in appearance. One of them, immaculately dressed in a neat grey suit and gleaming shoes, got out. He was inspecting the cattle yard when Caroline Klass first saw him from her cottage next door – yet in some uncanny way, he was instantly beside her, asking where Pauline Coombs was, somehow knowing that she, Caroline, was not Pauline. Caroline described him as speaking with a foreign accent and as having something 'alien' about him. He possessed 'large, penetrating blue eyes which seemed to go right through her and examine her thoughts.'

The report alleges that the Coombs' eldest son, Clinton, was in the neighbouring cottage at the time but was too frightened by the sinister visitors to open the door to them. Instead, he bolted it and hid upstairs. Failing to get an answer to his knock, the man returned to Caroline Klass and pressed her for further information, though he seemed to know her answers before she had even uttered them. Then he asked her to show them how to reach their next destination, and the two men set off in the strange vehicle. A few seconds later, Pauline arrived home in her car. Investigators commented on the fact that, although there was no turning off the lane by which she had come, Pauline had not passed the two men. How could she have missed them?

A strange entity,* below, *dressed in silver and with a black head, was also seen at the time by two of the Coombs children.

If things had indeed taken place as this report suggests, we would have good reason to believe that something genuinely uncanny had occurred at Ripperston. However, certain investigators have said that their enquiries revealed the 'evidence' to be a hotch-potch of misleading statements and mischievous inventions. There is nothing to suggest that the two men were foreigners, they say. They were not uncannily identical either; and what is more, their questions were perfectly natural. Far from knowing that Caroline Klass was not Pauline Coombs, their first action was to ask if she was indeed Pauline. Clinton was not hiding in the house, terrified. And as for the question of why Pauline Coombs had not passed their car as she drove up, the explanation is perfectly simple – Caroline Klass had pointed out a short cut that would enable the men to reach their destination more quickly, and it led away from the farm by a different road.

In short, the whole episode, as reported, is held by these investigators to be an irresponsible distortion, designed to create a sensational story out of a simple and perfectly natural incident. Moreover, they add, this was far from being the only west Wales sighting in which the true facts were somewhat different from those originally reported.

SAUCERS OF SATAN

WHAT IS THE PURPOSE BEHIND THE UFO PHENOMENON? SOME PEOPLE ARE CONVINCED THAT UFOS ARE ESSENTIALLY EVIL – THAT THEY MAY ACTUALLY BE EMISSARIES OF THE DEVIL, SENT TO POSSESS AS MANY HUMANS AS POSSIBLE

The typical UFO is frightening, or even menacing – as in this artist's impression of a demonic-looking flying saucer. Could it really be, as many writers have suggested, that UFOs are representatives of an evil power?

'UFOs are here to possess your soul!' Headlines such as this – from the American magazine *Official UFO* – are generally dismissed as coming from the lunatic fringe of ufology. Indeed, the theory that UFOs are controlled by demonic forces, seeking to delude or destroy Mankind, is often derided as just another crackpot suggestion, to be taken no more seriously than the idea sometimes put forward that there is a UFO base near the Welsh coast. But by no means all those who support the theory of the demonic origin of UFOs are eccentrics: indeed, there seem to be a number of realistic ideas that may point to a viable interpretation of the UFO mystery.

So what is it that makes a ufologist turn to theories of this sort? Is it merely that nothing else seems to fit – or is there solid evidence that really seems to point in that direction? Some commentators have suspected the former, while others have rejected the theory outright.

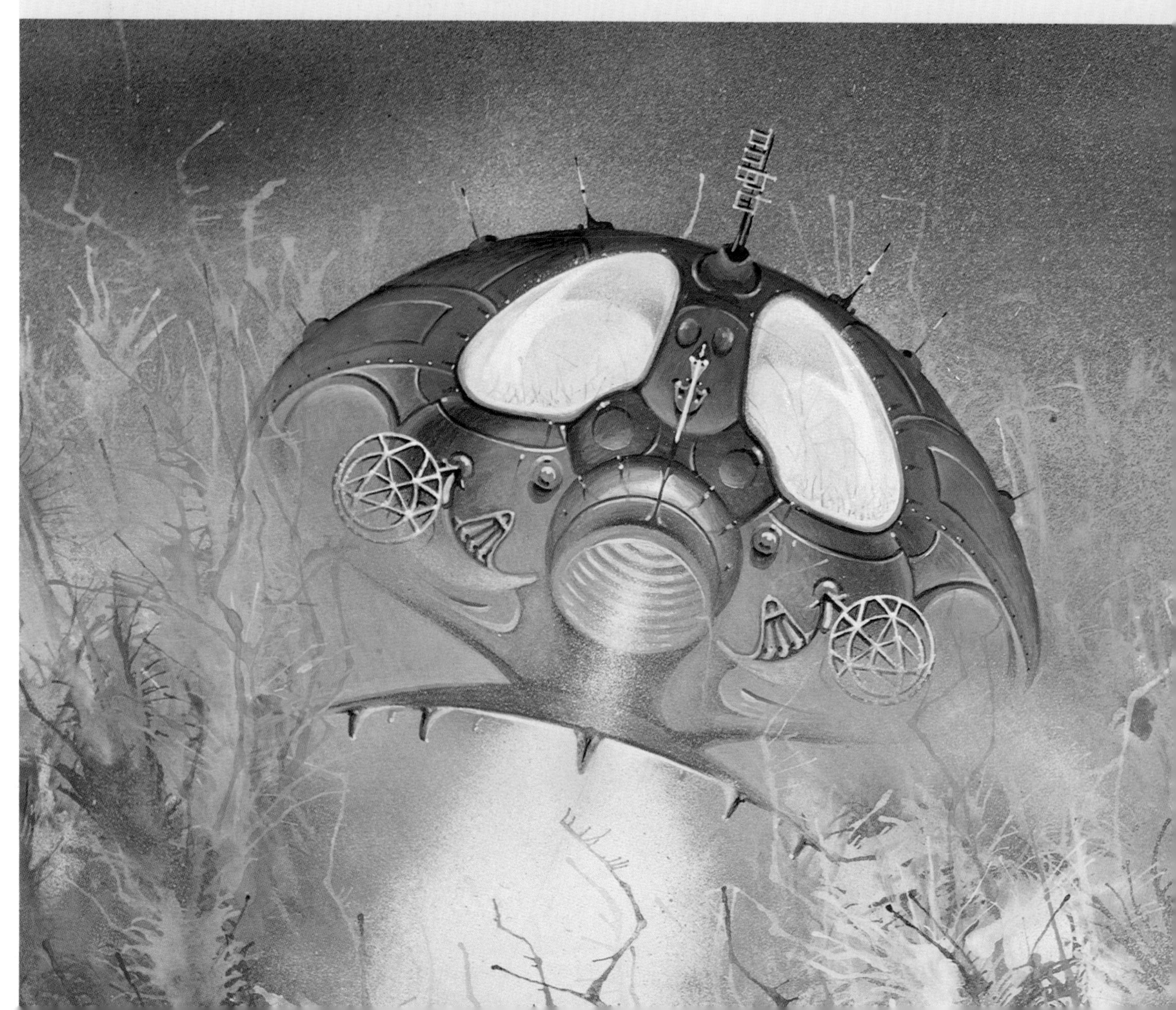

In their book *Flying Saucers are Hostile*, authors Brad Steiger and Joan Whritenour observed: 'Certain saucer cultists, who have been expecting space brethren to bring along some pie in the sky, continue to deliver saucer-inspired sermons on the theme that the saucers come to bring starry salvation to a troubled world. The self-appointed ministers who preach this extraordinary brand of evangelism ignore the fact that not all "saucers" can be considered friendly. Many give evidence of hostile actions. There is a wealth of well-documented evidence that UFOs have been responsible for murders, assaults, burning with direct-ray focus, radiation sickness, kidnappings, pursuits of automobiles, attacks on homes, disruption of power sources, paralysis, mysterious cremations, and destructions of aircraft. Dozens of reputable eye-witnesses claim to have seen alien personnel loading their space vehicles with specimens from earth, including animals, soil and rocks, water, and struggling human beings.'

Commenting in *True's New Report* on this horrifying catalogue, science-fiction author Frederick Pohl riposted:

'It's as false as false can be; there not only is not a "wealth" of such evidence, there isn't any. The absolute best you can say in support of that claim is that there are many people who think such things happen, and a mass of circumstantial bits and pieces of events. There is no evidence at all for the assumption that the saucers are almost certainly hostile.'

It is perhaps quite significant that even Steiger himself eventually backed down from his former position. *Flying Saucers are Hostile* was just one of the books that he wrote in the 1960s; others were entitled *Flying Saucer Invasion – Target Earth*, and *The Flying Saucer Menace*. But his *Gods of Aquarius* of 1976, subtitled: 'UFOs and the Transformation of Man', expresses the belief that 'the UFO will serve as the spiritual midwife that will bring about mankind's starbirth into the universe.' Cynics might suggest that Steiger, having milked the UFO-scare theme for all it can give, went on to find the positive approach more profitable; but

The illustration, above, shows UFO witnesses being brainwashed, and comes from the American magazine* Official UFO. *Supporters of the hypothesis that UFOs are demonic in origin cite in its favour evidence of physical and mental illness suffered by UFO witnesses after sightings. There is, however, an equally strong group of ufologists – among them* Frederick Pohl, left *– who have expressed the belief that the evidence is too slight to prove the evil origin of UFOs.

> "To me, the UFO, the appearance of elves and wee people and the manifestation of archetypal images throughout the world signify that we are part of a larger community of intelligences, a far more complex hierarchy of powers and principalities..."
>
> **Brad Steiger, Gods of Aquarius**

perhaps he genuinely changed his mind about the nature of UFOs.

However, there is no lack of continuing support for the demonic theory. But the crude business of rape and murder is not for the new demonists: what they fear is a more subtle take-over, aimed at men's minds or, for those whose beliefs include such a thing, their souls.

Alien Spirit?

In the Baptist Church at Warminster, southern England, on 28 January 1979, Arthur Eedle, physicist and astronomer, delivered a public address in which he told of his own personal encounters with demonic UFOs:

'In the summer of 1967, I was out watching for UFOs with a teenager by the name of Philip. As we waited in the dark, we became conscious that something was hovering silently overhead and quite near. I began to feel cold, more cold than seemed appropriate for the time of year. But Philip reacted badly to this thing, which incidentally we were only just able to make out, so low was its luminescence. He started to shake uncontrollably, and I realised that he was in some kind of danger. I bundled him into my car and took him home. We sat by the kitchen boiler and tried to warm up, but Philip could not recover from the shakes. The effect was no longer due to the cold, but to some induced effect from the UFO. I said: "Philip, do you believe in God?" "I don't know," he answered, "I have never given it any thought." I laid my hands upon his head and said: "In the name of Jesus Christ, I command this influence to leave Philip at once." The result was quite dramatic. Philip explained that a cold sensation travelled upwards through his body and out through my hands and away. Within a few seconds, all the shaking had stopped. Feeling a lot better, he looked at me and said that he now believed in God and the Devil!

'A short time later, Philip contracted the shakes all over again. I sensed that he was possessed of an evil spirit. Commanding this spirit to manifest itself, an old cracked voice spoke through Philip's mouth, saying that his name was Satan. I commanded it to leave in the name of the Lord Jesus, and it did so.'

Evidently, for Arthur Eedle, the Devil was very much a living reality. Further confirmation came from another UFO-related incident in the course of which he had a dramatic encounter with three fallen angels. They told him of their plan to take away men's minds and reduce them to 'a zombie-like state'. Identifying themselves as coming from the planet Martarus, they said they aimed to bring peace to the world by eliminating Man's destructive urges – which involved removing his soul entirely.

But this, Eedle claimed, is a pack of lies: 'They lie about their origin, saying they are from outer space; they lie about their purpose, saying they have come to help Mankind; and they lie about their identity, saying they are extraterrestrials.' In fact, Eedle insists, they are the fallen angels, based here on Earth where they are preparing for a final take-over that has been prophesied throughout history and is now imminent. He continues:

A terrifying alien with a huge, cabbage-like head, appears in a poster for the 1950s movie* Invasion of the Hell Creatures, *as seen* below. *Such movies have done a great deal to fuel the idea that UFOs are hostile.

'The present UFO activity points to the fact that these prophecies are on the point of fulfilment. People are already being brainwashed, and those many humans who are possessed of evil spirits have been prepared for the day of their coming. And it is clear that some of them are here already. The basic purpose behind all UFO phenomena today is to prepare for the coming of the Antichrist, and the setting up of World domination under the Devil.'

This is all very well – but before people can be brought to appreciate the mortal danger they are in, they must first be convinced that devils themselves are a reality. For most of us today, devils no longer form part of our system of belief. Evil is seen as resulting from distorted impulses in people's minds, rather than from some tangible external source. So the first concern of believers like Arthur Eedle is to reawaken the public to the fact that the Devil is actually real.

In a privately-printed booklet entitled *Who Pilots the Flying Saucers?*, Gordon Cove insisted that, by refusing to believe in devils, people will be laying themselves open to attack. In 1954, when the booklet was published, the majority of ufologists were inclined to interpret UFOs as physically real spacecraft, piloted by aliens from elsewhere in the Universe, rather than creations of the mind. Cove went along with this view, but at the same time gave it his own interpretation:

'What we are suggesting is the possibility that Satan has seized one of the planets as his base of operations to attack the Earth. This thought... may seem fantastic: but upon cool meditation, does it seem so absurd? The first thing a military general seeks, when war is declared, is a convenient headquarters. Satan is the cleverest military genius ever known. Is it feasible that Satan, along with his principalities and powers, his wicked angels and demons, would continue to float airily around in the atmosphere for thousands of years, when there are literally millions of planets which would be well adapted for a headquarters?

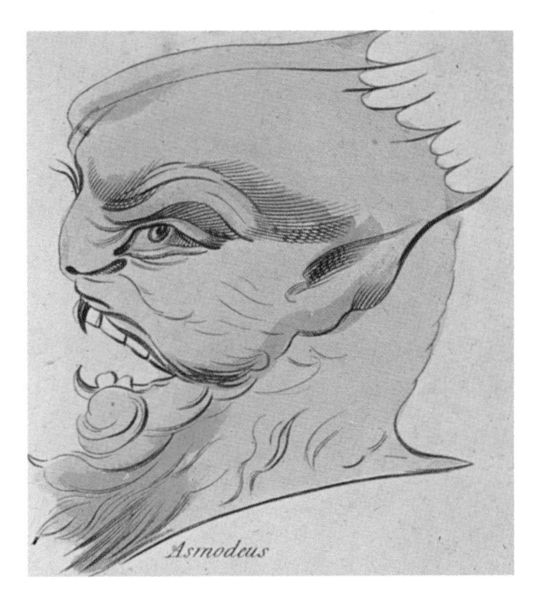

An illustration from Francis Barrett's* The Magus, right, *shows the demon Asmodeus who, in one of the stories of the Apocrypha, is conquered by the archangel Raphael. The face shows a marked similarity to those described by present-day witnesses of humanoids. It has been suggested by some writers that 'evil' humanoids are merely a kind of updated version of medieval demons.

'Satan is partially powerless unless he can get some willing instruments to work through. Therefore, if Satan wanted to manufacture some flying saucers in order to facilitate the flight of his evil hosts throughout the vast Universe, it would also be to his great advantage to get a race of beings under his control who would manufacture them for him. Could he not inspire the Venusians, if such exist, with supernatural cunning and wisdom to make a fleet of flying saucers, and also show them how to pilot these supernatural machines?'

Cove concludes that the beings who have contacted people with terrible warnings may have been 'demon-possessed Venusians or Martians', whose seeming benevolence was a sham.

However, he does not rule out altogether the possibility that some of the UFOs may be piloted by benevolent beings. The striking increase in UFO activity of recent years, according to Cove, must surely indicate that a full-scale attack by the satanic forces is imminent; and the forces of good must be aware of this. So some, at least, of the flying

INTERPLANETARY REVELATIONS

In his book, *Gods of Aquarius,* Brad Steiger tells the story of Ruth and Ernest Norman who first met at a psychic convention in Los Angeles in 1954. Ernest and Ruth immediately saw in each other shared ambitions, and consequently set about developing a life plan.

Ernest was convinced that he had been sent on a mission to this planet from a higher spiritual plane. Ruth, meanwhile, was eager to follow his teachings and aid his work, recording extensive channelled essays on the planet Venus. Finally, a series of 17 texts was published as a result of astral trips to that planet, involving what Ernest referred to as 'mental attunements'.

Then, in December 1971, Ruth reported, her husband 'changed worlds' and went back to a higher sphere, leaving his work in her hands.

Almost two years later, Ruth Norman was in psychic contact for a 10-day period with 32 other worlds. During this time, she apparently learned of the formation of a so-called Interplanetary Confederation which Earth would be invited to join. As a result, those of us on this planet would be able to learn what is going on elsewhere in the Universe and what others inhabiting the cosmos are like and capable of. According to Ruth, we will eventually learn how to travel from planet to planet, too, and transmit from higher dimensions an unlimited energy supply that will last for all eternity.

As Steiger was told: 'It is the prediction and will be the salvation of Man on Earth: so fear not the UFOs. They come near so that Man may see they mean no harm, but rather they are the only means by which the Earth people will be saved from themselves and their degenerative past... '

Interpretations of the purpose of UFOs, such as that illustrated* right, *vary from a heralding of the Second Coming of Christ to possession of our souls by the Devil.

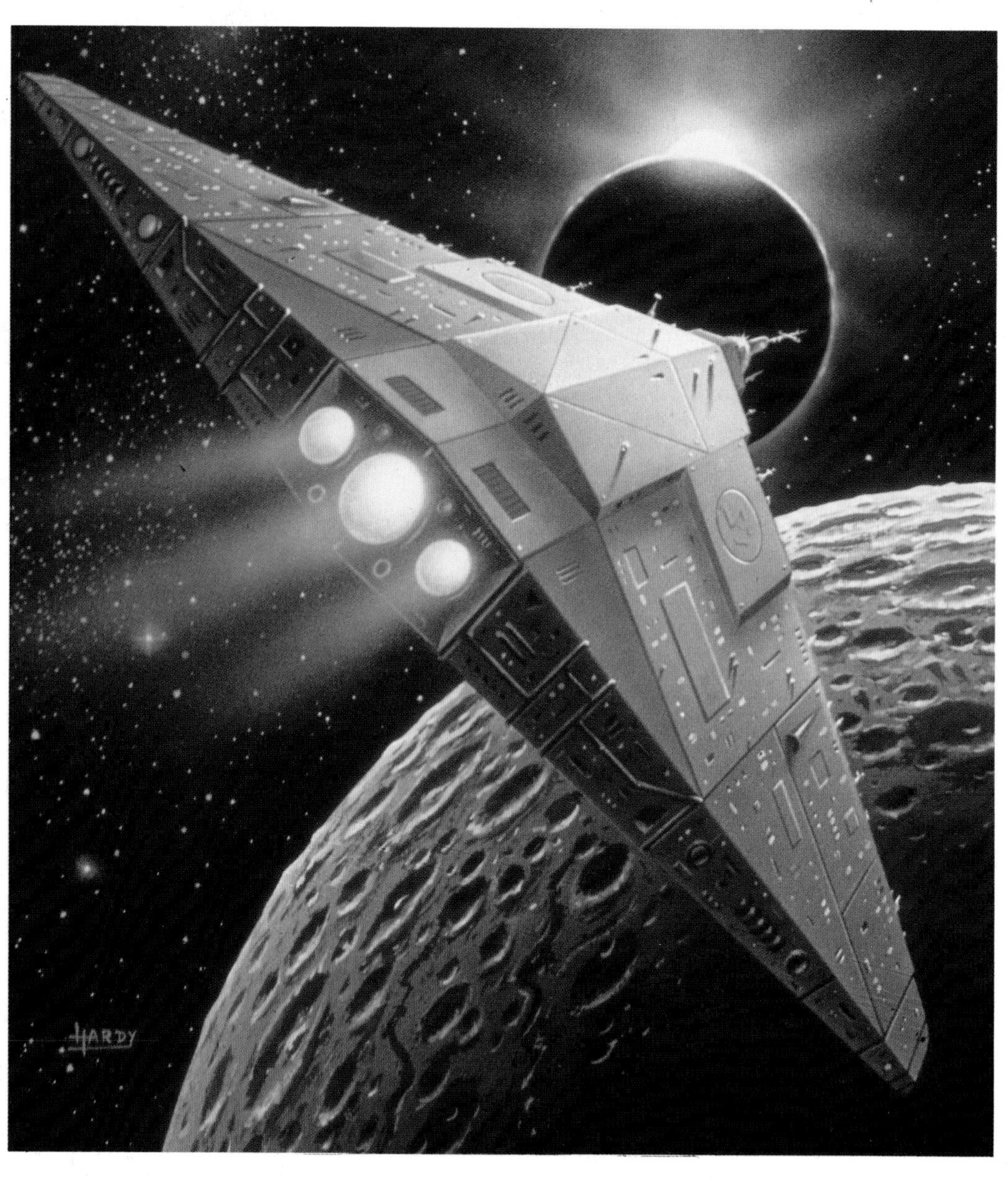

saucers may contain angels, sent by God to report on the state of the Earth.

'The question arises, what are the angels reporting to God after their tour of inspection? They cannot have failed to observe the awful tide of corruption and sin that is fast engulfing both the USA and Great Britain. Our sins rise up to the heavens like giant mountain peaks and literally scream to God to pour out his vials of wrath upon us!'

However, we may draw some comfort from the fact that Cove quotes a prophet named Hehr, to whom it was revealed, as long ago as 1903, that: 'A Third World War may wipe out our civilization, and that an older race on Venus is taking measures to re-establish a new and better order in the shortest possible time. When the atomic bombs fall, these extra-terrestrial aeroforms may be used to salvage what is good in our civilization, either persons or things.' And when is all this to happen? Hehr's target date for the start of the Third World War was 1960, and peace was to be re-established, after five years of chaos and total anarchy, in 1965!

However, even though we managed to escape that particular calamity, it does not do to be complacent: there are plenty more prophets with plenty more warnings of doom. Bob Geyer, of the Church of Jesus the Saucerian in Los Angeles, told the writer Eric Norman in 1970: 'Our conversations on the religious aspects of UFOs brought forth the conclusion that they herald the Second Coming of Christ.' But whereas Gordon Cove asserts that the UFOs are piloted by devils masquerading as alien visitors from space, Geyer takes an opposite view. For him, the UFO pilots really are extraterrestrials. It is we, here on Earth, who have labelled them as devils – not realizing that Satan himself is an alien, who has persuaded other aliens to join him,

'Satan, the old prince of darkness. and his legions of demons, are also beings from other worlds. They came down from another planet. Once, Satan was a member of God's astronauts. He became too greedy and too ambitious. He may have exploited the inhabitants of Earth, or other planets. He may have tricked people into slavery.'

The interpretations may vary, but the demonists are agreed on the main issues. Whatever the UFOs may be, they represent a menace to us on Earth; and the scale of their activity shows that menace to be imminent. But just what danger is it that they threaten?